dennis **wise**

dennis **wise**

the **autobiography**

B⬛XTREE

First published 1999 by Boxtree

This edition published 2000 by Boxtree
an imprint of Pan Macmillan Ltd
Pan Macmillan, 20 New Wharf Road, London N1 9RR
Basingstoke and Oxford
Associated companies throughout the world
www.panmacmillan.com

ISBN 0 7522 1719 4

3 5 7 9 8 6 4

A CIP catalogue record for this book is available from
the British Library.

Typeset by SX Composing DTP, Rayleigh, Essex
Printed by Mackays of Chatham plc, Chatham, Kent

To my wonderful Mum and Dad and sister, Kim, my niece Emma Louise and my lovely Claire, who are the most important people in my life.

Special thanks to Phyllis and the late Norman Edmonson, and their son Gary, who looked after me in Southampton and made me feel so welcome.

Thanks to Steve Stammers for all his great work on this book, Eric Hall, my friend and manager, Ken Bates, Colin Hutchinson and Chelsea Football Club who have helped me so much, and all the Chelsea players and fans.

Picture Credits

Childhood photographs: Dennis Wise
FA Cup semi-final: *The Informer*
Cork, Wise and Sanchez: Action Images
Wise and Hoddle: Press Associaiton
Wise, Waddle and Gascoigne: Stuart Robinson, *Daily Express*
England v. Turkey: *Daily Mirror*
England v. Nigeria: Dennis Wise
Wise with parents: Dennis Wise
Wise, Jones and Fashanu: Action images
Wise with Vialli: Dennis Wise
Wise and Sheringham: Dennis Wise
Chelsea v QPR: Dennis Wise
Wise in 'Cheer up Luca' T-shirt: Action Images
Wise and Gullit leading FA Cup team: Popperfoto
Wise with FA Cup: Popperfoto
Wise and Hughes with Coca-Cola Cup: Neil Barnett
Wise and Vialli with Cup Winners' Cup: Action Images

Whilst every effort has been made to trace copyright holders for photographs featured in this book, we would like to apologize if there have been any errors or omissions.

contents

chapter 1

the worst moment of my life

Footballers, particularly those like me who are lucky enough to play for one of the more glamorous clubs, have a great life. Don't let anyone kid you otherwise. You want tickets for a show? Someone will get them for you. You want to eat at the best restaurants? Someone will get you in when you want. You want to go to a night-club? Someone can arrange it – no waiting, no problem. You feel that nothing can touch you. You feel somehow totally protected. Then something happens to let you know you are just as vulnerable as everyone else is. No matter how much money you have, no matter how successful you are, you are still open to things outside your control. And that is exactly what happened to me on 13 March 1995. That day I experienced the longest and most terrifying one hour and fifty minutes of my life. It was the day I thought I was going to jail. It was the day that changed my whole approach to everyday living.

Five months earlier I had been involved in that row with a taxi driver. You might have read about it in the papers. At the time it seemed like nothing, just a minor row that had happened on a night which had started in very normal fashion with me and a couple of friends enjoying a good time at Terry Venables's club, Scribes. It was a Saturday night and it was all going well. We decided to go to a party over on the west side of London and we left the club to get a couple of taxis. Myself and the girl with me crossed the road and hailed a cab that was going in the direction of Hyde Park Corner. We had to go to Shepherd's Bush first to pick up a friend of mine called

Barry and then we were going on to Boston Manor.

We jumped in and the driver was fine about going to Shepherd's Bush but as soon as I mentioned Boston Manor he didn't want to know, 'Sorry, I'm not taking you there,' he said. I said that, as he was willing to let us in the cab to go to Shepherd's Bush, so now he had to take us on to Boston Manor. He told us to get out but I said, 'I'm going nowhere,' and refused point-blank to move. We had what you might call a right argument. As I saw it, he had his light on to say that he was free and had picked us up. But because we weren't going exactly where he wanted he ordered us out. But I wasn't going to budge just because we weren't the easy fare he thought we were going to be.

'Alright, if you won't take us to where I want to go, then take us to the nearest police station and we will sort it out there,' I said. I was confident of being within my rights to do that but he said, 'I'll tell you what, I'll take you to the East End and I'll drop you off there.' I told him he could please himself. He drove off quickly but suddenly braked. We both shot forward in the cab. The girl with me started to get out, he drove forward quickly again and she got caught in the door. I screamed at him to stop and banged on the partition window because I thought there was a real danger she would be hurt. The window smashed and I got him round the neck because I was so furious at what he had done. The police arrived and I was handcuffed and taken to the police station. It was a really miserable end to what had started out as a great evening. I had just been called up by England and that day Chelsea had beaten Leicester 4-0 in a league game.

The seriousness of what I was facing was brought home when I had to return to the police station two weeks later. I was told I was being charged with causing criminal damage and assault. I was sick to my stomach when they said that. I had been to police stations and in court before. But on those occasions it was for drink-driving offences. I'm not suggesting for one minute that that's clever. It isn't. But this was different. I had to give my version of what had happened in an interview. Everything was very formal and not at all friendly. And there was the first mention of the possibility of prison. Now that does frighten you. You don't think an argument that went a bit too far can lead to that.

The following day I reported for England duty. That evening, the FA's public relations man, David Davies, came into my room saying there was a problem. Suddenly this five-minute ruck was becoming something major. He said that the story was coming out in the *Sun* the following day. I saw Terry Venables and he was great with me. He said there was no problem as far as he was concerned. He also said that the press wanted to speak to me the next day and, although I was reluctant, he persuaded me to do it.

Leading up to my first appearance in court in February, I wasn't too worried. No one wants to go to court but my legal people had assured me that, if I pleaded guilty, I wouldn't be going to jail. It was more likely that I would get community service – maybe 100 hours – and a big fine. But I thought about it and decided against pleading guilty. Why? Because I reckoned the taxi driver was partly to blame for what happened. I might have reacted more than I should have done but someone with me had been hurt and in those circumstances you do things to protect your own. That's how I was brought up anyway.

So as far as I was concerned, he didn't help the situation and it wasn't all down to me. I shouldn't be pleading guilty and he shouldn't be getting away with it. So in went my plea – not guilty. I gave my evidence, so did he and so did the police. But I did have some reservations going into court. It wasn't so much about my innocence or guilt. As I said, I didn't think I was guilty. No, it was because of the timing. I was worried that the authorities would make an example after the recent Paul Ince and Eric Cantona incidents at a Crystal Palace v Manchester United game. Cantona had reacted to insults thrown at him by a Crystal Palace fan and had dived into the crowd with the infamous 'karate kick'. Ince was charged later after another incident in the same match. Neither had gone to prison but I didn't feel all that secure because of it. It seemed to me there was a distinct danger of someone trying their best to make an example of a footballer that they reckoned had stepped out of line and I had this nagging feeling that it would be me. I was right, as well.

It seems to me that the better known you are, the more of a target you are. I often get fierce verbal abuse during games but I never see anything happen to the people giving it. I sometimes get hassled when I am out but nothing happens to the people who are giving that hassle. It just seems to me that people who are well known never get the benefit of the doubt and that often the authorities want to make an example of you. Frank Leboeuf and Franco Zola have told me that in France and Italy, if there had been a case similar to mine, the police would have given me the benefit of the doubt. But they didn't over here. I know people from my childhood who have been to court on several occasions for what are more serious offences than my row with the taxi driver and they have been given community service.

When the judge gave his verdict, guilty on both charges, I was gobsmacked. The judge told me that I would have to come back on 13 March to hear the punishment. The effect was immediate. It was decided that I would be left out of the England squad for the match against the Republic of Ireland. Suddenly all this wasn't going the way I was assured it would. The worst was to come, though.

When I went up to hear the sentence I was still convinced that all I would get was a fine or possibly community service. From what I had been told and advised, the prospect of going to prison never came into the equation. It soon did, though, and I can't tell you how horrified, shocked and distraught I was. When the magistrate, Geoffrey Breen, started talking it was like he was speaking to someone else, 'Three months on each count, to run concurrently.' I didn't even understand what concurrently meant. It is not the sort of word you hear every day at a football club training ground. All I knew was that I didn't want to spend one day in jail, never mind three months.

My legal people asked for bail and he refused. Then they went to Southwark Crown Court to appeal against the sentence and the conviction and hoped to get unconditional bail. But it was like all this was happening to somebody else, not me. I remember thinking, 'Just what is going on here? I was told I would be walking out of the court no matter what and here I was going down to the cells.' No way would the magistrate give me bail. I was in the loneliest spot in the world. In short, I was terrified. All I could hear was my legal people telling me beforehand I would be out and all I could see was two policemen saying that I had to go with them down to the cells.

I remember going through this huge iron door and walking down these stairs? Then one of them said, 'Do you want a cell on your own or with other people? Actually, probably better on your own, don't you think?' I answered by saying that I didn't want to go into a cell at all and said, 'If it's alright, I'll sit outside. I don't need to go in that cell, do I?' I wasn't being flash and I wasn't suggesting I was too important to be put in there. Nothing like that. 'I mean, I won't cause any trouble or anything like that if I sit outside. I promise.' Basically, I just didn't want to go in that cell. When they looked at the state I was in, I think they were a bit worried I might cause them a problem. I wasn't going to, though. I just didn't want to go in there. In my mind it was like a huge mistake. I kept thinking, 'What is going on here? This has all gone too far.' All the police said was, 'Sorry, you have to go in a cell.'

A community officer then came down and I asked him what would happen next. 'What happens now,' he said, 'is that you have been sentenced to prison and that is where you are.' I answered, 'I thought I was going to get community service,' and he said, 'That is what he should have given you.' I was worried, confused and upset. How could all this be happening to me? Then my brief came down and I said, 'Look, you have got to get me out of here. It has all gone too far.' He explained they were going to a higher court to ask for an appeal but that it had to be done by 2 p.m. that day. 'Or what?' I asked. The answer was not what I wanted to hear. 'Otherwise they will take you in a van to Brixton prison, maybe for a couple of days.' I was terrified.

All sorts of things went through my mind. Since the conviction the month before, I had been receiving all sorts of sick mail and faxes. The threats were clear and explicit: if I went to jail, I was going to be raped, beaten up and probably both. They upset me before but I didn't give them much thought because I had been told all along that I wouldn't be going to prison. Now I could recall them all too vividly. It had all the makings of a nightmare becoming reality. At first those threats were laughable; now I was nearer to crying than laughing. It was the unknown that was frightening. I remembered going to see a pal of mine in prison. I took his girlfriend along so she could see him. I couldn't believe the state he was in – a busted nose and two black eyes. He had dropped some water or something and the screws had given him a right seeing-to. It was his first time in jail and they wanted to make sure he wasn't coming back, so they really gave him a going-over. The idea was to make prison such a horrible experience that he just wouldn't allow himself to go back and would steer clear of trouble in the future. It was supposed to be a dreadful and painful deterrent. He was sitting there, crying his eyes out. I was petrified that would be me in the next couple of days.

I thought, 'Sod this, I don't need it.' I began to think that even my football career would be in jeopardy because I had a nasty thigh injury and there was no way I would get the proper treatment in prison. I began praying that I wouldn't get put away. At Chelsea I would sometimes moan if I had to go in to get treatment on a day off – suddenly that treatment seemed a pretty good idea to me. It's funny the things you complain about, just silly things really. Then you have something really important to contend with and very soon you develop a keen sense of perspective.

That cell was the loneliest place on earth. It was cold. It was desolate. This woman, the duty officer, looked through the hatch every now and again to see if I was alright but she said nothing to me. I kept asking what was happening but she just blanked me. She was really cold – very aloof and very stand-offish – but I accept now that she had to be like that with her job. One of the police officers brought me a cup of tea and an apple and I asked him the same question I'd asked my brief, 'What's going on, what's going to happen?' 'Simple,' he said. 'You go to Brixton and you do your three months.' I remember going back to the seat in the cell, sitting there and just putting my head in my hands and thinking, 'What are you doing here, Dennis?' And, yes, I was tearful. I was scared. I am not ashamed to admit it.

It dawns on you how lucky you are outside. You feel you can basically do what you want, have a joke and get away with it and that nothing will ever happen to you. Now all this was out of my control and I was not used to it. I realised that I could lose everything through five minutes of madness.

That two hours I had in the cell was the longest of my life, no question. I was shaking and forever banging on the door, just wanting to know what was happening. And they kept saying the same thing, 'If you are not out of here by 2 p.m., you're going to Brixton.'

At eight minutes to two the court received a fax. 'Dennis,' the policeman said, 'you are out.' The appeal was granted and I was out on unconditional bail. I was shaking with relief. It was all so emotional when I saw my family, my agent Eric Hall, and my close friends Andrew Dale and Vaughan Ryan. I started crying – lots. I see nothing wrong in owning up to that. You have no idea the emotional turmoil I went through. It is such a scary situation when you don't know what's going to happen to you.

Up until then, whenever anything had gone wrong, I was able to fight back. Like the time when Southampton let me go as a player or if I was ever in a tight corner on a football field. This time I was in the hands of other people. For once in my life I wasn't in control and that made me panic, it made me anxious. I was totally reliant on somebody else and I felt so helpless. I never ever want to be in that position again. I want my fate to be in my hands, not someone else's.

Over the following weeks I got plenty of hassle from the media. The pressmen were everywhere – at my house at Gerrards Cross, and I just didn't need it after what I had been through. They were even at my sister's house, banging on her front door all hours of the day and night. That really got to her because she had just had a baby. And there was still the appeal process to deal with and I had no idea what the outcome would be. It was still possible that I would end up in prison and that filled me with dread, I can promise you. Now I knew what less than two hours was like, how could I face two or three months? The thought made me shiver.

Glenn Hoddle was the Chelsea manager at the time of the incident. When I got back to the club after the court case a few people asked me if I had seen him and I said I hadn't. Then Hoddle said he wanted to have a chat with me. We were standing out in the middle of one of the pitches at the training ground at Harlington. He said, 'I need to tell you that I'm going to take the captaincy off you.' I asked for the chance to explain what had happened from my point of view. He just said, 'No, I have made my decision and that is what I am going to do. I am going to take the captaincy away. I feel this is what I have to do.' He didn't let me explain or, in fact, say anything and all I could say was, 'Fair enough. It's your decision. Please yourself.' I just walked away. But I was really disappointed that he wouldn't listen to me. That hurt. I love being Chelsea captain; it's one of the greatest honours I've ever had.

But the club were great. When I got sentenced, they decided to intervene and help me. It was all going wrong for me at the time. As well as the threat of prison, I had a bad thigh muscle injury that stopped me from playing. While the appeal was being prepared, they made sure they got me on the treatment table. Although that was good, not playing matches meant that I had no diversion to distract me from the threat of prison. Before that, getting out on the pitch was an escape from all that was happening. I could leave all the problems behind in the dressing room and I could lose myself in football. It was two hours of escape. Now I didn't even have that.

I was given a choice of dates for the appeal, April or June. I chose June because, if the sentence was upheld, I could do my time during the close season. I think that's what Glenn and the club wanted.

Some important evidence came our way before the appeal was heard. I don't think the taxi driver, Gerald Graham, wanted the matter to go as far as me going to prison. I think he just wanted money, some kind of compensation for the aggravation he had suffered. He had submitted an invoice at the original court case. But when I saw what he was claiming for now, it was incredible: new handbrake, new window, new upholstery, new bumpers . . .! Basically, he was claiming for the complete refurbishment of his cab. But I had hardly done any damage, and when a new invoice was compared to the first one the difference was huge. His lawyers thought I would just pay it without comparing the two. But they were wrong and the discrepancy was spotted. That was bound to count in my favour; it was a godsend.

Then there was the issue of a pair of glasses. He said in the original claim that I had broken them. But when photographs of the damage inside and outside the cab were taken, there, on the back seat, was a pair of glasses – the ones I was supposed to have broken – looking, as far as anyone could see, in perfect condition.

The conviction was overturned at the appeal. The most worrying time of my life was over. But I never want to go through anything like it again and, believe me, I won't. Some lessons never leave you and I can assure you this was one of them as far as I am concerned.

Through it all the players at Chelsea were great. And I have to thank Craig Burley in particular. When I was back at the club waiting for the appeal in June, the first few days were awkward. People were a bit wary of what to say – you know, acting very edgy and not wanting to say the wrong thing at the wrong time to upset me. I would have been the same. It was Craig who broke the ice. While all the players, including me, were sitting at the table at the training ground one lunchtime, he said, 'Right, I've had enough of this. Who wants to hear about Wisey in Brixton Prison?' He then proceeded to tell the following joke. To many it will seem a bit crude but you have to remember this is football club humour. Humour is such an important factor with a squad of players – it's like a safety valve to get rid of the tension. And it really helped to eliminate the tension around me and the rest of the squad.

'Okay,' said Craig. 'So Wisey starts his three months in jail. He is led down to the cell and the screw beams this big smile as he locks the door. Wisey looks round and there at the other end of the cell is this six foot, eight inch guy standing by the wall. 'Hello Dennis,' he says, 'I am your room-mate for the next three months. Now shall we sort out who's going to be mummy and who's going to be daddy?' So little Wisey thinks on his feet and decides that, if everything is in proportion to the guy's height, then he will be better off being daddy.

'Okay,' said the guy, 'That's fine by me. Now come over and give mummy a blow job!'

I know it sounds awful but it's the kind of banter that is part and parcel of life among players. And to be fair, it was like clearing the air and the jokes started coming thick and fast. Little John Spencer was one of the worst, always asking if he could have the use of my BMW while I was inside. I couldn't complain at being the target. I'd pulled enough stunts myself. Thankfully, it all came out well for me in the end.

But there were plenty of moments in my career when I didn't think it would.

chapter 2

childhood

The area of London that I grew up in, around Shepherd's Bush and Notting Hill, was tough. Basically, you had to learn to look after yourself. It doesn't help if you are accident-prone . . . which is exactly how I would describe myself. Not clumsy, but if anything was going to happen to anybody it would happen to me. If someone was going to get knocked down by an ice-cream van it would be Dennis Wise. If anyone was going to fall off a tree over in the park, it would be me.

I can think of two true examples that summed up how it was for me as a kid. We were living on a council estate in Shepherd's Bush and there was a road into the part where our houses were arranged in a circle. I was about 12 or 13 at the time and my parents had just given me a chopper bike. I was with my sister Kim and a couple of mates, Victor and Barry, and we would have time trials around the square to see who could go the fastest. But it was important that you slowed down when you came to the side of the road leading into the square, in case there were cars coming.

But one afternoon I wanted to win so badly that I didn't bother stopping because I thought it would gain me a few extra seconds and that would enable me to win the race. The problem was that there was a car coming up the road and I shot straight over the bonnet. Thank God I was alright – but then I saw the driver getting out of the car . . . it was my dad. My mum was in the car with him and she got out and was going mad with worry. Then my dad saw it was me and just shouted, more with relief than anger, 'You silly bastard!' Me? I just got up and ran home as quickly as I could.

Another time Kim and I were playing with a tennis ball up in my mum and dad's bedroom. The ball ran under their bed and I crawled underneath to try and find it. It was too dark down there to see anything, so Kim had an idea. She ran downstairs and got my mum's cigarette lighter. She flicked the lighter and the flame caught the underside of the mattress. It proceeded to go up in flames with me underneath. I was struggling to escape the flames when, thank God, my dad came in, lifted the bed up and freed me.

My dad, Dennis, was a painter and decorator before he and my mum, Pam, took over a pub, and they made life as good as they could for Kim and me. Both my parents were West London people and they married when they were 19. I was born on my mum's 21st birthday. Mum was as strict as she could be and tried to keep me out of trouble, but it wasn't always easy. I remember her catching me playing truant once. I was with a gang of mates who had skipped off school to miss the PE lesson. She stopped her car, wound down the window and asked me where I thought I was going. When I said we were going round my mate's to get his PE kit, she didn't believe a word and made me go back to school. She gave me a right telling off when I got home that evening.

The council estate where I was born was pretty run down but at least there were plenty of places to play football. I was always mad keen on football and it was in the blood too, because my dad used to run a kids' team called Bellevue. With Dad running them I was able to do what I loved doing best most of the time – play football. He taught me a lot, and although he ran the team and I played for it, he wasn't in any way biased towards me. If anything, the opposite was true. He was the other way where that was concerned and made me work even harder than the others. He was always on to me to improve and, although I may not have appreciated it at the time, I was a better person for it.

At that time my team was Queens Park Rangers because my hero was Stan Bowles. He was a good friend of my dad's and one day, when I was about seven years old, Dad brought him down during a training session for Bellevue. I had a kick-about with Stan and then had my photo taken with him. I prize that photograph to this day. It was amazing for me to meet a real footballer and he really showed an interest in what the Bellevue lads were doing. To me that showed a lot of thoughtfulness and it made a big impression on me. Stan immediately became my favourite player and, because he was at QPR at the time, they became my club.

I really enjoyed those years with my dad's team but I was already showing signs of the competitive streak that was to get me into such trouble in the years to come. It first showed when I was seven. I was playing for the Under-11 team and we were involved in a six-a-side tournament. Our club produced the two best sides in the tournament. We both got through to the semi-finals where we played each other. It was the A team against the B team and I was in the A team. We thought we were the bee's knees and it was a real crunch game. They beat us; I was devastated and acted like a real spoiled brat. I thought we should have beaten them and gone through. Their captain – a lad called Dave Cracknell – came up to me at the end to shake hands and I threw a moody and walked off. My dad saw it and came storming over. 'Get yourself here!' he screamed and, when I got there, he gave me one almighty clout round the ear. Then he made me shake Dave's hand. And it got worse: the B team went on to win the final.

That was a lesson I learned but nothing changed my attitude about wanting to win. I hated losing. I did then and I do to this day.

When I was young football was the only sport in which I had any interest. In my first year at secondary school – the Christopher Wren school in Acton – we had to play rugby and football was banned. I would frequently miss PE, which didn't interest me, and rugby which I hated. When we moved into the second year, we moved to another part of the school, in White City. And it was there that I first met someone who was to become one of the most expensive strikers in England – except in those days Les Ferdinand was the goalkeeper for the school team. I think he played there because he wasn't too keen on running about. He was a very quiet bloke and didn't say much at all. He was very placid and it took a lot to rile him. But that didn't mean he couldn't handle himself if someone went too far – as I saw for myself.

There was a bully in our year who started to pick on Les. He probably thought the same as the rest of us – that Les hated trouble and confrontations and would do nothing about it. One day he went too far and it was probably the worst mistake the fellow ever made. Les proceeded to absolutely batter him. He had the whole year cheering him on as he laid into this bully. After that Les was everyone's hero and he was also the bloke no one dared to upset any more.

Our school team was doing alright at the time and, when I was 12, I got noticed by the Southampton scout in the London area, a man called Bob Higgins. I was asked to go to their training centre in Slough, and my mum and dad would take me twice a week. It was good there. I really enjoyed it. At 14 I was old enough to sign for a club on associated schoolboy forms. A few clubs were keen on me: Queens Park Rangers, Tottenham and Chelsea all wanted me to sign for them. But I had been happy in the Southampton set-up and I had made some good mates at the centre. I didn't see any reason to move, so I signed for them.

Two years later it was time for apprentice forms. A couple of London clubs offered my mum and dad money for me not to stay with Southampton and to sign for them. I won't say which clubs they were, or how much they offered, because what they were doing was strictly illegal. In those days, officially, if the club that had you on schoolboy forms offered you an apprenticeship, you had to take it. But despite the rules it was easy to get out of if you wanted to go elsewhere. You just had to say that you were homesick or something.

Anyway my parents told me about the approaches from other clubs and explained the situation. I knew the money would be more than handy for them but they said all along that they wanted me to go where I wanted to go. If all my mum and dad were interested in was money rather than my welfare, they could have picked up a tidy sum. But I said I was happy at Southampton. So Southampton it was.

During that time, I had been noticed by the England schoolboys' team. But my chance of appearing for the team disappeared after a train journey I took with Tony Adams. We were part of a group of 28 who had made it to the final trials for the England team. We were all 15 years of age and there were about half-a-dozen of us travelling up to Lilleshall for the last stage of the selection process. Tony was with us as was Michael Thomas, who went on to play for Arsenal and England. Six of the 28 were to be left out – and we went some way to helping the selectors make up their minds!

On the train we started to mess about. It all got a bit loud and one of the lads started throwing crisps about. Then one had a mock fight with me. There was nothing serious about it all, just a bit of laugh. But one of the passengers got annoyed by our antics and came over to ask us to keep the noise down. He saw that we were wearing blazers with school badges and said he would report us when we reached the end of the journey. One of the lads just said 'F . . . off' to him as he walked away. It so happened that the man was a headmaster and when we were getting off the train he went up to one of the ESFA officials and told him what we had been up to and complained about our behaviour. He said we had been a disgrace and there was no way in the world we should be allowed to represent England at anything.

Anyway, the trials went ahead and I had really high hopes that I would be selected for the final 22 – but the six of us got letters saying we would not be selected because of our behaviour on the train. Actually, Michael Thomas had his punishment rescinded after it became clear that he had nothing to do with the fooling around, but it was a major disappointment to me that I didn't make it. To this day I have no idea whether I would have got in on the strength of my performance in the trials. But the decision was made based on my behaviour and it was a lesson for me, at a very early age, that when you are representing England you have to maintain standards of behaviour. It was a huge blow to me and my parents because I had high hopes of breaking into the schoolboy side. But they were more disappointed than angry with me.

I now know that getting away from the Shepherd's Bush area did me a massive favour. From the age of 14 or 15 the kids I was hanging about with were starting to get into trouble. There were a group of us who went around together and, though we were not hardened villains or anything like that, we just wouldn't let anyone take the mickey out of us. I started getting into fights inside and outside school. Eventually I was suspended from school for two weeks for fighting. I was due to go to Southampton as an apprentice the following August and the school thought it might be a good idea for me to go early. Even though I was 15½ and hadn't taken my exams, the school thought I would be better off in Southampton. They spoke to the club and and they agreed to take me early.

To be honest, I think there were several teachers who were glad to see the back of me. In physics I used to walk into class and the teacher would say I could go if I wanted. I didn't need to be asked twice. They knew that all I was interested in was football, not schoolwork, and they were worried I would get into more trouble if I stayed with the same gang of kids. There was every chance of that as well.

When you are young, you are impressionable. You just do what the others do for a laugh. You think you are just enjoying yourself and it is so easy to get into more and more trouble. There is always the danger that you can get into a life of crime and a few of the blokes I grew up with did just that. I was lucky. The chance came to get away and move to Southampton and, as much as it helped me in a football sense, it took me away from an area where I could have landed myself in trouble with the police. As for all the fights I was getting into at school and away from it, well all I can say is that where I grew up you have to learn to stick up for yourself.

My last night at home was a sad one. My mum and dad arranged a leaving party for me and all my mates. The kids I had grown up with came along to wish me all the best. I felt really sad afterwards at having to leave everything I knew behind me. I moved into digs in Southampton and I was on the road to becoming a pro. Or so I thought . . .

Chapter 3

southampton

Life in Southampton won't go down as the happiest period in my life, but not because of anyone down there. The family that I first lived with in 1982 – Kay and Don – were smashing. Although it was a well-disciplined home, I felt really at ease there. I have some lovely memories, like having my picture taken with Kevin Keegan and meeting people like Peter Shilton and Alan Ball. But quite simply I was homesick. My parents used to come and watch me play on Saturdays and I would go home with them. And instead of going back to the digs on a Sunday night, I would get the first train back on Monday morning to give me an extra night at home. Although the family were great, I couldn't help but feel just a bit lonely at times.

Sometimes the frustration would show out on the training pitch and there was one occasion when I clashed with a bloke called Steve Baker. I was only 16 and he was 26. He was a stocky little right-back and we clashed in a training match. The ball was played to me and when I held it up he kicked me from behind, so I elbowed him. As I started to run with the ball he clipped my heels and I stumbled. I carried on but slowed down to let him catch me up. Then I turned round and just whacked him in the face. We started fighting and had to be separated. All the older pros were laughing because there I was, only a kid but standing up to one of them. Before we were parted he headbutted me and I was sent down to the dressing room with this huge bruise on my head. I didn't want him to think he had hurt me, so, as I had long hair at the time, I pulled it down to cover the bruise.

Because I was an apprentice the next thing I had to do was clean his boots and take them to him. When I did, all the other pros were taking the mickey out of him, saying how he couldn't even beat a 16-year-old kid. In the end he was alright about it but the whole thing really got me down. I rang up my mum saying I was fed up and wanted to come home. It wasn't the best atmosphere with the reserves because the older ones didn't like kids coming along and taking their place in the team. Basically, the club do that to give the youngsters the experience of playing against men, but the older ones, in their mid-twenties, didn't see it that way. They resented it.

But it wasn't only on the pitch that I was getting into bother. There were one or two occasions away from the club when I found myself in hot water, like the night I went out with one of the senior players, Reuben Agboola. I was only 17 and he was a good bit older than me and on this occasion about nine of us apprentices went out with the older pros. I went to get a hamburger and when I came back I saw three or four blokes laying into Reuben. I didn't even think to find out what had happened – I just ran over to join in and help him out. This was outside a night-club in Southampton and what had apparently happened was that Reuben had a row with his wife in the club. He threw her out and her brothers came looking for him. But none us knew this at the time and we all steamed in to help him. A lad called Ian Baird, I remember, was with me and it was all going off outside the night-club. Reuben made a dash for it across the road and was hit by a car.

It was in the papers a few days later, and the fact that an apprentice – me – was involved was a main part of the story. Lawrie McMenemy, the manager of Southampton at the time, was told about it. There were other apprentices there but I was the only one who got into trouble. He fined me two weeks' wages and sent me home. It wasn't my last time in trouble with him either.

The discipline down at Southampton was great, probably the best at any club I have played for in my career. Everyone had their jobs to do – clean boots, clean the baths, clean the dressing room. All had to be done and done properly. It usually went well. In my second year I was the head boot boy, which basically meant I was in charge of handing out jobs. I made sure that me and my good mate Ian Straw got the best job that summer – cleaning Lawrie McMenemy's car on Fridays. It was a cushy number . . . outside in the sunshine for a couple of hours instead of cleaning little bits of metal in the showers or bath. That used to drive me mad.

But being in charge brought about another summons to see Lawrie. One day I told this huge guy Mark Blake, who was about six feet one inch tall, to clean the baths. He said he'd done them. I said they hadn't been done very well and he would have to do them again. Then I said that if he didn't I would put him in the bath. He refused and started to walk away. I grabbed him by his shorts and threw him in the bath. I just said: 'Now clean it!' As I walked away he grabbed me round the throat and started strangling me. Ian Straw and a couple of other lads tried to stop him but because he wouldn't let go I sunk my teeth into his arm and bit as hard as I could.

Then came the trouble. Blake had gone to one of the coaches and said I was picking on him. He showed him his arm and a scratch on his face. Next day, we were called in to see Lawrie McMenemy in his office. He walked straight up to me and said, 'Do you want to be a bully?' I said, 'What? How can I bully someone who is more than six feet tall when I'm only five feet seven?' But before I could say anything else he had me by the throat and up against the wall saying, 'Bully me, come on, bully me!' He said the same thing to Ian Straw but I said Strawie had nothing to do with it. I said I had the fight with Blake because he wouldn't clean the bath. But he would have none of it. He said he was sending us home and that he didn't know if he wanted us back. He said he would think about it.

They took us back after two weeks and I changed digs to live with another lovely family, Phyllis and Norman Edmondson. Their son Gary was like a little brother to me and it was only because I was so happy with them that I stayed at Southampton. I was really fed up with everything that was happening. But a little while later I was moved into different, really strict digs where you had to be in by 10.30 in the evening. A minute or two late and the man would really get on to you. It made me feel even worse.

When the time came to sign as a professional I spoke to a lad at the club called Eamonn Collins who was six months older than me. I reckon he must have told me a few lies about what he was earning. So when Lawrie offered me £100 a week to sign for Southampton, I said it wasn't enough. He raised it to £125 a week in a two-year contract. Then I asked for a £250 signing-on fee and that was it. He just told me to get out. I went back to see him because I had to tell the club formally whether I was going to accept the offer. I said I was rejecting it, packed my bags and went back to my digs. I'd had enough.

I rang my mum and told her what had happened. I was crying and she said she and my dad would be down as soon as they could. When I said goodbye to the family I was staying with I was really rude to them because, to be honest, I don't think they treated me very well. They were always going through the things in my room. I had no privacy. I hated it there and it was the greatest feeling ever to go home.

But now I had no money coming in and, because Southampton had my registration, I couldn't sign for anyone else. First I went down to QPR and trained with them. They were impressed in the week I did down there and they wanted to sign me. That was fabulous news and a great relief. It meant I would be earning again. But the manager Frank Sibley told me there was a problem – Southampton had my registration and someone would have to pay a fee for my release. Frank said that, while he would like to keep me, QPR had no money. I was shattered and, although my parents were brilliant and said they would help me, it was an awful feeling having no money. I was supposed to go down and sign on the dole but I couldn't go through with it. I couldn't bring myself to do it. I was too proud. It was like I had been beaten. I was really conscious of the fact that I was among the people I grew up with and there was every chance they would see me down the dole office. I would have been seen as defeated and I would have felt humiliated if I had been seen by any of them. After all, it hadn't been that long ago that I had a big farewell party for Dennis Wise, the professional footballer-to-be.

After QPR I went down to Crystal Palace. Steve Coppell was manager then but he was away for a couple of weeks and his assistant Alan Smith was looking at me. He said, after a couple of days' training, that he thought I was a decent player and one of his coaches, someone called John Griffiths, was saying that Palace had to sign this kid Wise. But Smith said there could be no decision about signing me until Steve Coppell came back. But I couldn't wait a couple of weeks. I needed a club and I needed to get involved in football again straight away. The end of the season was coming and if you haven't got a club at that stage you could be knackered during the summer.

It is funny how things turn out because a year or so later Palace were very keen to sign me. By then the fee would have been £1 million, which was too much. But I remember John Griffiths saying that Palace really had let me slip through their fingers. They could have had me for much less a year earlier.

I got home from Palace and there was a stack of phone calls from people involved with Southampton – Bob Higgins, Dave Merrington and Lew Chatterley. They all said the same thing: ring Lawrie McMenemy, apologise and ask to come back. I was so fed up because no one wanted me that I swallowed my pride and rang him. I said I was sorry for turning down the contract and, if it was still on offer, I would like to sign. He replied, 'Pack your gear, get your mum and dad to bring you down, leave your gear at the digs and come and see me.' I thought my career at Southampton was back on track and we did what he said. After dropping off the gear, my mum and dad waited in the car outside The Dell while I went in to see him.

I went upstairs, knocked on his door went in and said, 'Hello, Mr McMenemy.' He just handed me my registration. He made me do all that just to let me know I had no future at Southampton. But I shook his hand and thanked him. At least now I could sign for whoever might want me. There would be no money involved and that was a relief. But who was going to take a chance and pay money for a kid who had been nowhere near the first team? Because of what had happened to me at Southampton, some people might have doubted my temperament, so it would have been really hard to persuade someone I was worth a gamble. I went back in the car, collected my stuff from the digs – again – and the next day was the first of the rest of my life.

Chapter 4

the gang assembles

Not long after I'd left Southampton for the final time, I got a phone call from Pat Dellar, a scout for Wimbledon. He had recommended me to the Wimbledon manager Dave Bassett, Harry, as everyone calls him. Pat asked me to come for a two-week trial and after I met Harry, he said he'd let me know one way or the other if Wimbledon wanted me to stay. No messing me about. That's what I wanted to hear and agreed to go down there without hesitation.

The day after that Gwyn Williams from Chelsea – now the assistant manager at Stamford Bridge – rang to ask what I was doing. I explained the situation with Wimbledon and he said, 'Well, as far as I'm concerned, you can't become a bad player overnight and, if it doesn't work out, come down here.' Well, it did work out. After four days of the fortnight Harry said, 'I want you to sign.' He gave me £90 a week and I was delighted, absolutely delighted. I had my self-respect back because now someone wanted me for their club. It was such a contrast. When I first came back from Southampton I wouldn't even go out because I didn't want people to see me. Everyone on the estate knew that I had gone off to be a professional footballer and I was back home a failure with no money and no club. Now I could hold my head up again.

It was towards the end of the 1984-85 season and Wimbledon were safe in the old Second Division from relegation, so Harry named me in the squad for a match against Cardiff. I was sub and I came on to set up the winner. I felt fantastic to be playing as a professional. Harry promised me that, if I did well the following season, he would give me a better contract and he was as good as his word.

It wasn't that comfortable at Wimbledon at first, though. The reserve manager Geoff Taylor didn't really want me there because he wanted to push the kids that he had brought through, players like Andy Sayer, John Gannon and Andy Thorn. But I was determined to make this chance count. What I had experienced at Southampton helped me. When you are young and you feel that you have been a failure it gives you extra drive and incentive. When you get another opportunity, you work that much harder. I was taught a big lesson at Southampton and it gave me a fright, a huge fright. I realised that, without football, I would be lost. I hadn't any plans or qualifications for anything else. I didn't take exams at school because all my energy had been directed at becoming a professional footballer. But no one could have predicted what was to follow or the adventures that would come my way.

That summer, Dave Bassett decided he wanted to toughen me up. He had been pleased with what he had seen but, because I had been playing mainly in the reserves against players of my own age, he wanted me to have some experience of playing against men. So he arranged for me and another young player – Sean Priddle – to play in Sweden during the summer. We really looked forward to it because it was like a holiday and, as well as being paid £150 cash in my hand as wages, the club – Grebberstad – gave us a flat and a car. Grebberstad were battling against relegation from the Third Division at the time. The manager was a really nice bloke called Ben Mathieson – I used to call him Bonce for short – but he wasn't too impressed when he first met us.

Neither of us was particularly tall and he told us later that he took one look at us and wondered how we would survive what was a really physical type of football. But we did. I played up front, off the centre forward, and scored six times in 12 games. And they stayed up. Sean was in midfield and he did really well, too. When it was time to go back to England, Bonce said he would love to have us back any time.

But we never went back, the standard wasn't very good. But the loan spell had served it purpose – both Sean and myself had experienced playing in really physical football. We also had the benefit of learning to look after ourselves away from football and that is a key part of the growing up process. We benefited from that. I know Sean did – he's a millionaire now!

When I went back to Wimbledon, it was basically to reserve-team football. I played only four first-team games that season and my full debut was against Sheffield United in 1986. It was not one to remember in some ways, though. We were 5-0 up and won a penalty. I took it – and missed. Nevertheless I was settling in well at Wimbledon and enjoying living with my family again. My mum and dad were able to come to every home game and a good few of the away ones as well. I was making new mates at the club too. I got close to Vaughan Ryan and Andy Sayer, but particularly Vaughan. I am still mates with him now.

And once Harry had signed me as a full-time professional, you have no idea how special that made me feel. I didn't have to clean any more boots for a start. I didn't have to wash out any showers or clean any baths. All those crap jobs that I hated having to do when I was an apprentice, they were now in the past. All I had to do now was what I wanted to do all my life . . . train for and play football.

John Fashanu had been signed in the summer of 1986 from Millwall for £125,000 and there were good players starting to come through the ranks – Andy Sayer, Andy Thorn, John Gannon and Dave Beasant was in goal. And we had Alan Cork, a terrific character and player who I believe was very underrated. Very dry, very laid back and a very good player. He loved it when I was in the team and reckoned that if I had been alongside him five years earlier he would have made a fortune because of the goals he would have scored. We just had this telepathy between us. He knew exactly where I was going to put the ball and he would invariably get his head to it. Among the players he was a father figure to me.

At Wimbledon we were a collection of lads with something to

prove. The majority had come up through the lower divisions, the youth system or non-league – or even, like myself, from the prospect of the dole queue. None of us had much money and most had been released by clubs at one time or another during their careers. Maybe they had trials or just hadn't been taken on. But we all seemed to have something in common – a hunger to make a living out of football. We all had something to prove, to ourselves or to the people who had told us at various times that we wouldn't make it in the professional game. That is a very powerful driving force. There was a great camaraderie among us, a fantastic spirit. Because we had been given another chance to make the grade in the game we loved, we worked hard but we all enjoyed ourselves in the process. And we all owed a lot to Dave Bassett.

Harry was a terrific manager, one of the best I have ever known. From my first day at the club he made me feel so welcome and he instilled into us the same kind of togetherness that you would normally associate with a Sunday morning team. It was under Harry that we were given the nickname of the Crazy Gang and that stemmed from the kind of things he used to have us doing as much as the kind of things that we used to get up to as a squad of players. For instance, while most teams were going away on their pre-season tours to Scandinavia and Germany, we used to be training at army camps near the south coast. The idea was to toughen us up and make us that bit harder for the challenges of the season. And you would have to say it worked. After a week or 10 days at a barracks, regular training didn't seem so bad!

Harry was great at making the training sessions a laugh and quite often we would finish up with a game of American football or maybe a rough and tumble game of British Bulldogs on a Friday. There was no midday meet before a home game either, not for Wimbledon. Harry wanted us there by 1.30 for a 3 o'clock kick-off and I would say the majority turned up at 1.29 . . . with the rest arriving a minute later!

That kind of spirit filtered through to the players and the managers that followed Harry. I mean, Bobby Gould drove a mini-bus carrying our kit to White Hart Lane when we played our FA Cup semi–final there in 1988. How many other managers have done that? I reckon we were also the first to introduce ghetto-blasters in the dressing room as a way to make us relax and psych ourselves up for matches. The opposition must have been wondering what bunch of nutters had moved into the dressing room next door.

Then there were the initiation ceremonies for the new players. When John Hartson joined Wimbledon, a lot was made of him having his Armani suit cut up by the players, but it was just a kind of traditional welcome. It was Harry's Crazy Gang who started those traditions. Eric Young was one particular victim. Eric was a really hard central defender who had joined us from Brighton. He was proud of his kit-bag which had the name of Brighton on it. It was his pride and joy and clearly meant a lot to him, he loved it . . . and that made it the most natural of targets for the rest of us. One day we had a ceremonial burning of it in the middle of the changing room at the training ground. He was furious at first and went potty but he calmed down in the end. It was just the Wimbledon way of things.

But it wasn't just about initiations for newcomers; we were constantly playing tricks on each other. Players would often go into the car park after training to find the tyres on their car had been let down and another favourite was to smear Vaseline over the windscreen. Car racing after training was another regular feature, and it was not always a day of celebration if it was a player's birthday. After training, whoever it was would be stripped and have black polish applied to his . . . well, let's call them 'naughty bits', and then he would be carried out and left in the middle of the training ground – which, by the way, was a public park. The lady at the training ground who washed the kit was June Ryan, Vaughan's mum, and I reckon she must have seen about 50 or 60 lads run in stark naked. Upset? No, she just used to burst out laughing.

We had our share of characters at the club and one of the biggest was John Fashanu. There was no doubt – he was the top man. Basically, what he said went. Fash was a strong person with a strong personality.

When Fash had something to say, we would listen. I suspect that a few of the older professionals there resented him a bit at first because of the influence he had at the club but the majority of the players looked up to him.

But Fash was one hell of an asset for Wimbledon. He was a record buy for the club and had this air of being born for something better. He was really well spoken and articulate. He had all these businesses outside the game and he was the club personality of the time. But he was one very hard man – as a player called Robbie Turner found out a few years later. We had bought Robbie from up north and he was a front man who liked to play in Fash's position. He let other people know he should be in the team ahead of Fash, and Fash got to hear of it. One time, we were in the dressing room – Vinnie Jones, Fash, Robbie and me. Fash just said, 'Jones Boy, shut the door.' He did and Fash turned on Robbie. Fash said, 'I hear you have been putting yourself about a bit, so let's sort it out.' Robbie agreed – and suddenly they started fighting. Me and Vinnie just sat there gobsmacked. Fash slaughtered him and Robbie conceded defeat. Fash had made his point. Luckily for me, I got on really well with Fash from the start, and with Vinnie Jones, who became one of my best mates.

In my experience, Vinnie and Fash are two of the nicest people I have ever met and the three of us always seem to get together, even though we've gone our separate ways. We were together again at the premiere of the film *Lock, Stock and Two Smokin' Barrels*, in which, of course, Vinnie had a part. As we stood there, Fash said, 'Look at this. It just goes to prove what I have always thought that no matter what, the three of us – Ratski (his name for me), the Jones Boy and Fash – we will always be there as mates. It can be good or it can be bad, but we are always there.' That was a nice little reunion.

Back in the days when we were players together, Fash always seemed destined for some kind of success. He was high-profile and I had always had him down as someone who would do well for himself. You have to remember that he didn't start with a silver spoon in his mouth. Just like the rest of us at Wimbledon, he came from humble beginnings – in fact, more humble than most of us because he was brought up in Barnardo's. He had to battle and scrap for everything in life.

Vinnie was the same. He was a hod-carrier playing for non-league Wealdstone before joining Wimbledon for £15,000. I got on well with him from the moment that he came to the club and we played in the reserves together. What I do remember is that he was very raw. He had this drive and determination and in truth couldn't believe his luck that he was now being paid to play football full-time after all those years on the building site. His enthusiasm was incredible and he would run all over the field like a nutter. He was incredibly strong, could get from one penalty box to the other and was not afraid to put his foot in. Over the years he has had his critics but I can only talk about Vinnie as a team-mate and I am telling you he is someone you want on your side. He was another one with something to prove and he set about that from day one at the club.

He gave everything in training and in matches. Quite simply, he ran his heart out. Me and him were always at the front in the three-mile runs we used to have. I had a bit more pace, so I would invariably beat him to the line but not once did he give up. The one thing we did have to change about him when he arrived was his haircut. It was a real rascal, very curly and just like a perm. I am sure he is glad he changed that!

Before Vinnie made his first-team debut against Manchester United in 1986 he was very nervous. You have to remember that a few months earlier he was getting up at 6 o'clock every morning to work on the building site. Now he was going to face Manchester United with Bryan Robson and all in their team. Some contrast. Vinnie may have his limitations, but he is as brave as a lion and he went out and not only played a decent game but scored the goal in a 1-0 win. If Vinnie felt he had something to prove then he proved it that afternoon. He was just so delighted afterwards. I know how he felt. It really means something when you have had so many things go wrong in your bid to be a player and suddenly it all comes right. His confidence grew after that day and rightly so. And he went on to become a Welsh international.

A lot of people have knocked Vinnie over the years. They keep harping on and on about what he can't do, what he is bad at in the game. All I can say to that is look at the clubs he has played for since joining Wimbledon. Among them are Leeds and Chelsea. Look at the money that has been spent on him over the years. You don't spend that kind of money on people who can't play.

It seemed that people couldn't wait to have a go at him, saying he couldn't play. Well, I have been in the same team on many, many occasions and take my word for it – he could play. He was strong as an ox, tackled for fun and could really get a team motivated. He also scored more than the occasional goal. He had a real presence in the team and his sheer determination helped him have a really decent career in football. He was also a very down-to-earth person and still is. Me, him and Fash used to socialise a lot and, although we were often in West End clubs, Vinnie was always more at home in a pub. That was his scene and quite often he would go down my mum and dad's pub – the Bridport Arms in Notting Hill – and ring me to insist I join him for a drink.

That was typical of Vinnie, and typical of the down-to-earth attitude at Wimbledon. There was a real 'all in it together' feel about the team. Any trouble on the field and you knew you wouldn't be on your own. Fash, Glyn Hodges, Andy Thorn, Brian Gayle, Wally Downes and later Vinnie – they were all there to back you up. What Harry had done was assemble a group of players not with chips on their shoulders but with something to prove. I had my bad times at Southampton, Fash had come from Millwall, Vinnie came to us later that season from Wealdstone and Nigel Winterburn had been released by Birmingham. And in the 1986-87 season that gang was taking on the First Division. After our promotion everyone in football assumed that the Second Division was our level. No one took any notice of us. But although we didn't have an exceptional team, we played our own brand of football and it was effective. They weren't going to be able to ignore us for long.

Chapter 5

crazy days

Wimbledon were in the First Division in the 1986-87 season, and the big boys were in for a real shock when they came to Plough Lane. It was just like a non-league ground with awful little dressing rooms. The pitch was the only decent thing about the place. The glamour clubs hated playing there. It always seemed to be cold and you could tell they just didn't want to be there. It was like an away tie in the third round of the FA Cup for most of them.

Nobody was giving us a chance, so we all decided to just try and enjoy it. Not that we started all that well. Our first game was at Manchester City and I played. There were 20,000 in Maine Road and that was a huge crowd compared to what we were used to. We were beaten 3-1 but no one felt that despondent. We actually played quite well. A few days later came our second game and our first win, against Aston Villa at Plough Lane. I remember the Villa coach trying to reverse down the road to the ground. It's a poxy little road with a sharp turn in it and it's very easy to miss. It's right by a pub and the glamour teams must have been wondering what they were doing there. The dressing rooms are close and the other team would have been able to hear Fash winding everyone up before they went out on to the pitch.

We beat Villa, went on to win four matches on the trot – I scored my first goal to beat Charlton – and that put us top of the table, much to everyone's surprise. Suddenly we were getting a lot of media attention, people wanted to know about this team who shouldn't have won a game all season, never mind be top of the league. We weren't pretty but we were pretty effective. Nothing frightened us – not Old Trafford, not Anfield. We knew we were never going to win the league and all we wanted to do was stay up.

Soon stories began to leak out about Wimbledon's Crazy Gang, about the pre-season army training camps and about how we used to trash each other's rooms all the time. It all helped with the image and other teams were never certain what was waiting for them when they came to play us. We made the most of that. Having the ghetto-blaster music in the dressing room would drive other teams mad. And we had Fash doing his pre-match antics. Fash had a fantastic physique. He looked really fearsome when he stripped off, all muscle, not an ounce of fat. Anyway, at home games he used to just put a towel round him and walk down the corridor as the opposing team were coming down. It was a very small corridor and people would have to try to push by him to get into their dressing room. It was a tight fit and he would just stare at them, eyeball-to-eyeball. It was an intimidating sight. Vinnie joined us three months into the season and he would join in the ritual and stand alongside Fash. They made a fearsome duo and opponents didn't know what to make of it. It definitely gave us an edge.

After going top, the inevitable happened. We hit a bad run and dropped to 14th. Harry was a bad loser and that was no bad thing. But he did lose his temper and throw cups and things about at half-time. No one argued with him. But he was also a bubbly type of character who would always try to keep things going. He certainly had some funny ways, like when he was going to drop you. It was the same scenario every time. He would call you over, put his arm round you and offer you a Polo mint. Then he would say, 'You aren't playing this week.' I once asked why and he said, 'The truth is, Wisey, because you were crap last week.' There was no answer to that!

But he had everyone's respect. He knew how he wanted us to play and we used to work all the time on set pieces. We played the percentage game, the more times we got the ball into the opponents' penalty area the more times we were likely to score. Yes, we were physical; you can't be anything else with Vinnie in the team. I remember later that season when we played Arsenal Vinnie was given a specific job – and it didn't work out too well for him I'm afraid.

Steve Williams, an England international midfield player, was playing for Arsenal at the time and he was playing well. He was making them tick and Harry had singled him out as the danger man and the one who had to be stopped. He told Vinnie, 'I don't mind you getting sent off as long as Steve Williams goes with you.' Vinnie was still very raw and said he would do as he was told and ask no questions. But this time he got his instructions wrong. During the game he ran past Graham Rix and suddenly elbowed him. He was sent off straight away and Harry went potty. 'What the f . . .ing hell did you do that for?' he screamed at Vinnie afterwards. 'I thought it was Steve Williams,' said Vinnie. I just cracked up at that. How he got them confused I will never know. It is not as if they even looked alike.

A really big game that season was when Manchester United came to Plough Lane in the league. Liverpool had already been, but there has always been a ring about Manchester United coming to your ground. They were special and we beat them. It was Vinnie's debut and he scored the winner. What a feeling! We did really well against the bigger sides that season. We won at Chelsea and Liverpool as well as beating Manchester United. But then we'd lose at home to the likes of Luton and draw at home with Oxford. The games we should have won we didn't but the games when we should have been making up the numbers we won. That was the pattern for most of the season. The small clubs like us would fight like us and they always did well. The glamour clubs with the star names didn't like the way we played and couldn't handle it. They detested it when they had to play Wimbledon. And how they hated that ground. No matter how many people were there, it always seemed full.

When we won at Anfield that year, Vinnie summed up the lack of respect and fear we had for places like that. So many teams are beaten before they go on the field, but not Wimbledon. Vinnie made sure they knew it. Underneath the famous 'This is Anfield' sign, which is above the tunnel as you go out on to the pitch, Vinnie stuck a note saying,

'Like we are bothered'. When they came to us, he had another sign put up which read, 'This is Plough Lane'. It showed we weren't scared of reputations and I think the Liverpool players were a bit taken aback by that.

We had the same approach at Tottenham and won there. Tottenham always seemed to look down on us and they probably didn't want us in the league at all. The one time they did really battle was in the FA Cup game that season and they beat us with goals from Chris Waddle and Glenn Hoddle. But, to be fair, they did defend brilliantly that day.

But whatever the competition, we never worried, ever. If you don't play with fear, then you never get nervous. And we had a good few laughs on the way – like the time we tried to send the club owner, Sam Hammam, into the boardroom at Old Trafford in a shirt with no sleeves. He came into one of the rooms at the hotel we were staying in before the match at Manchester United and saw me doing this trick. It entails emptying a glass of water turned upside-down using a pen – of course, you can't touch the glass with the pen. What you do is take everything out of the pen so it leaves a tube, then you blow down it, the glass moves and the water comes out. But Sam couldn't see how it was done. So me and Vinnie Jones struck a bet with him. If we lost we had to get off the coach and enter the ground wearing just our pants. Actually we said we would do it naked but Sam insisted we kept our pants on. But if he lost, me and Vinnie would each rip one sleeve off his shirt and he would have to go into the boardroom like that. We gave Sam 30 seconds . . . and he couldn't do it. So we showed him how, and duly took the sleeves from his shirt. He was supposed to go in there like that, in what was left of his shirt. But the chairman Stanley Reed made him put a jacket on top. Shame, it would have made quite a sight.

And it all made for an incredible first season, the one that was also supposed to be our last. Instead of the nailed-on certs for relegation we were never lower than 14th and we ended up in sixth place. We proved that we could handle the top flight and all that went with it. We won at Liverpool and Tottenham and did the double over Manchester United in what was Alex Ferguson's first season. We also reached the last eight of the FA Cup, losing to Tottenham at home after beating Everton in the previous round.

But there was a far from happy ending to the season when Harry, the manager who had built up the Crazy Gang, announced he was leaving. He told us at the last game of the season at Sheffield Wednesday. It was a real bombshell and I took it badly. We were all gutted, me particularly because I owed him such a lot for bringing me back into football when I thought my chance had gone. He never gave us a reason, just said he was off. Mind you, I was only a young lad and he was never going to explain what he was doing to me. I begged him to stay but all he said was that I had done really well and to keep it going. It was a sad day and a sad journey home. It spoiled what should have been a terrific season.

Harry had been given the chance to go to Watford to take over from Graham Taylor who had taken the manager's job at Aston Villa. But nothing could make us feel better, nothing. I thought about all the great times that we had that season, particularly winning at Manchester United and the celebrations afterwards. For a small club we had made remarkable progress. It is even more remarkable when you think of the quality players that came out of that team: like Andy Thorn, Dave Beasant and Nigel Winterburn. Not to mention players in later years like Terry Phelan, Keith Curle and John Scales who went on to become internationals and were sold on for an awful lot of money. Not bad for the Crazy Gang.

Chapter 6

the fa cup campaign – 1988

So Harry was off, and to be truthful a lot of the players wanted to go with him. 'If you get the chance, buy us and take us with you,' was the message from many of us. He took two – Glyn Hodges and Mark Morris – and then Nigel Winterburn was also on his way at the end of that season, to Arsenal. Three key men had gone and I knew it was going to feel very strange starting again at Plough Lane the next season. There were changes on the coaching side too. Alan Gillett went with Harry and Gerry Francis went to Bristol Rovers after working with our defenders for a season.

Before then we had our end-of-season outing to Magaluf in Majorca – except that we were more like a Sunday morning team going to Margate. We went for a week and all I can remember is us getting scooters, wrecking the scooters and then getting drunk every night. Nothing was ever said to us about our behaviour because basically no one knew who we were. You wouldn't read about us in the papers because we were nobodies.

When we came back, nothing had changed in terms of facilities. We still trained on Richardson Evans, a public park in south west London. That somehow seemed right for Wimbledon football club – training on a public park where people are walking their dogs. It was good in a way because it stopped anyone getting carried away with their own importance. You can't really, if you are in a public place where anyone can go. But that sums up Wimbledon. Get ideas above your station and you get slaughtered.

It was decided that Bobby Gould was going to take over from Harry. He's a good man, I liked him straight away. The first time I met him he called me 'The Rat'. He explained that he had heard that was my nickname and he was going to stick with it. It was always plain Wisey or The Rat from then on. The first thing I noticed about him was that he had these huge eyebrows that met in the middle – and I remembered someone once said to me that you should never trust anyone whose eyebrows were like that. But I liked Gouldy from the start, especially since he doubled my wages from £150 to £300 a week.

Of course we had our rows – and fights. And I mean that literally. In his second year, the season after we won the FA Cup, I was making a right nuisance of myself because I wanted to leave the club. Bobby got really sick of it and called all the lads round to watch. 'Let's get this sorted out once and for all – now! Come on, hit me, hit me,' he kept saying. So I did. I gave him a right dig in the ribs – and broke one of them. He kept it quiet for weeks although he must have been in agony. He just didn't want anyone to know I had hurt him. But that was typical Gouldy – if there was a problem he would want it sorted out. He wasn't afraid of a public row.

He was the sort who would throw cups around in the dressing room and generally go potty when we lost. But it was clear that he had a passion for the game and he wanted us to share that passion. He also had the habit of making great signings from the lower divisions; players who cost virtually nothing but went on to earn millions for Wimbledon. And there were also experienced players like Terry Gibson, who had been at Tottenham, Manchester United and Coventry, clubs who clearly felt he had his best days . . . but Gouldy knew they were wrong. He was a great judge and would travel hundreds of miles every week to watch players. He bought Terry Phelan, Clive Goodyear, John Scales and, in 1989, Keith Curle. But his best signing, in my opinion, was his first: Don Howe. What a brilliant coach and motivator, the best as far as I am concerned. He played a huge part in our FA Cup success.

Gouldy was very unpredictable – he'd do or say the opposite to what you expected. But I had a lot of time for him and he certainly did well for me when he was manager. He seemed to pick up the Wimbledon way of doing things straight away. You know, the 'one in, all in' philosophy. He liked that because it showed spirit. But he wouldn't let you get away with stupid things. In one match against Charlton I ran 60 yards to get someone back and gave him a real kick. While he wanted us to be competitive he wouldn't stand for us doing something stupid, so he pulled me off straight away. I was fuming. I wanted to stay on but he gave me a right rollicking in the dressing room. He wanted us to get stuck in but not like that. He said he took me off because one more stupid tackle like that and I would have been sent off – and that would have been the team down to ten men.

He was very strong-willed – and that is just what you need to be if you are manager at Wimbledon. I thought it would be difficult to replace Harry Bassett but Gouldy was the perfect man to come in. He knew what was required.

Ironically, our first game of that season was away at Watford – Harry's new club. I missed that one and the next against Everton because of a suspension from the season before. We lost at Watford and drew against Everton. Everyone was saying this was the season Wimbledon would go down. You would have thought they would have known better. We picked up well after those first two matches and moved up to fourth in the table. We were never out of the top ten from mid-November onwards. But at Wimbledon, we always knew that if we were going to win something it was more than likely to be one of the cups. We went out of the Littlewoods Cup (the League Cup) against Oxford, so it was on the FA Cup that we focused our attention.

The squad of players we had in 1987-88 was probably the strongest that Wimbledon have ever had. It was a shame that we had to break up after winning the FA Cup but it is almost inevitable at Wimbledon. It just can't be avoided. If we had managed to stay together, there is no telling how much more we might have progressed and achieved. The FA Cup run started against West Bromwich Albion – and a row with Ron Atkinson, who was their manager at the time. I scored a real screamer from 30 yards but, as I hit it, one of their players caught me late. It really hurt and, in true Wimbledon style, the rest of our team were forming a queue trying to get him. The West Brom players went mad when I hobbled off. And when I came back after a few minutes, Atkinson had a real go at me, accusing me of making the challenge look worse than it was. Anyway, we won 4-1 and, although I can't really explain it, we all just felt this could be our lucky year.

In the fourth round, we were away at Mansfield and I came across a player who was later to be a team-mate at Chelsea – their goalkeeper Kevin Hitchcock. He was already at Chelsea when I joined and his first words to me were, 'You're the little bastard who stamped all over me in that cup match.' He had a good memory. The ball came in, he came out and I lunged for it two-footed. He went mad at me – until he looked up and saw Vinnie Jones and John Fashanu there to back me up. Our motto at Wimbledon was simple, 'Take one of us on and you take us all on.' The team were particularly protective of me because I was small. Anyway, we won 2-1 although we needed Dave Beasant to save a penalty in the last couple of minutes. Mind you, he owed us that. After Alan Cork had given us the lead, Bes made a terrible rick to let them back in the game. He went to clear the ball, missed it completely and the ball bobbled over his foot to leave their striker with an easy chance. I had set up our first goal for Corkie and then Terry Phelan scored our second to put us back in front. Bes made amends with his penalty save and we had survived a tricky tie. A lot of First Division teams would have been put off by their horrible little ground but it didn't bother us. It was better than we were used to at Plough Lane!

Next up in the fifth round were Newcastle and, as usual, people assumed we were just there to make up the numbers. It was Newcastle's year – everybody said so. They had Paul Gascoigne, who was coming through as a real character and real talent. It was also a match with history. When we played the league game at Plough Lane two weeks earlier, there was the infamous incident between Gazza and Vinnie Jones. Vinnie had been told to mark him but Gazza made him look silly with a nutmeg and then ran past him. He made him feel even worse when he then bent down and looked through his legs at Vinnie. A real mickey-take. But you didn't do that to Vinnie without expecting – and getting – something in return. Sure enough it arrived. No one knew what to expect but we knew something was on the way and it came when Vinnie was standing in front of Gazza and suddenly put his hand back to grab him between the legs. It was caught on camera and the photo was shown everywhere. We all knew it hurt because Gazza really squealed.

Afterwards, Vinnie was informed in no uncertain terms that he would be sorted out when he came up to Newcastle for the cup game. It seemed that everyone on Tyneside was out to do him we were even threatened when the team coach arrived at St James' Park. It bothered Vinnie not one bit. We knew he could handle himself. He handled the situation brilliantly and kept Gazza quiet – a great achievement on his home ground. We won comfortably 3-1. John Fashanu, Terry Gibson and Brian Gayle scored for us. Newcastle relied on Gazza and, though you could see back then he was going to be one hell of a player, we handled him well.

So we were through to the sixth round and a home game against Watford. It should have been Harry Bassett's new club against his old one, but by then Harry had left Watford and Steve Harrison had replaced him. That day was the first time that we really thought we could actually win the FA Cup. At half-time we were a goal down and we had Brian Gayle sent off. If you are going to lose, then that is the kind of game in which it is going to happen. But Eric Young equalised and then John Fashanu got the winner. We really rode our luck that day and came through.

The semi-final draw was so, so kind to us. There were two really good teams left – Liverpool and Nottingham Forest. Wimbledon and Luton made up the last four. What we didn't want was one of the first two – and we got Luton. I felt we had a great chance of winning. Not that Luton were a bad side but they weren't in the same class as Forest or Liverpool.

The match was at White Hart Lane and it wasn't the greatest. But what do they say? Semi-finals are for winning, not for remembering. They went ahead through a player who was later to join Wimbledon, Mick Harford. But we didn't give up. They had two more decent chances but didn't take them and gradually we came back into the game. Luton, under Ray Harford, were well organised but we worked ourselves three one-on-one situations with their goalkeeper Andy Dibble. We missed the lot. Then we were given a dubious penalty. Terry Gibson was brought down by Dibble and to this day I am not convinced it was really a penalty. Put it this way, I would have been upset if it had been given against us. But the referee gave it and I nearly cost us the equaliser. John Fashanu was getting ready to take it, probably the most important penalty in the club's history. He was wound up enough – what he didn't need was me coming up to him and saying, 'Fash, don't miss. Please don't miss. You can't miss.' He just told me to sod off . . . or words to that effect. He was under enough pressure as it was. I couldn't bear to watch. But he showed nerves of steel and tucked it away.

Our confidence grew and we really began to think we could win the game. And we did – with me getting the winning goal. It came from a long throw, a flick down the line and Alan Cork hooked the ball over. I managed to get in front of Tim Breacker and slid the ball under Dibble. The emotion of the moment got the better of me then. I just got up and kept running, and running and running. I wasn't running anywhere in particular. All the lads were trying to catch me. The first person I saw was Terry Gibson and he was standing on the halfway line with his socks rolled down. I just jumped on him and the rest of the lads piled on top. I looked at Gibbo's face and he was nearly crying. It must have meant a lot to him because he was a former Spurs player and this was his greatest footballing moment – and it came at White Hart Lane.

The tears really flowed at the full-time whistle. The worst affected was Alan Cork, who had never won anything in his life and was in the FA Cup final. He had nothing to show for all his years in the game and now he was off to Wembley. It really got to him. And as we sat in the dressing room afterwards we were beginning to think what it meant – me included. Typical raggy-arsed Wimbledon, we came to the semi-final of the FA Cup in our own cars with the kit arriving in a mini-bus. It was just three years before that I was on the football scrapheap. It seemed like just the day before when I was too embarrassed and proud to sign on the dole – and here I was in the FA Cup final. It was too much to take in and none of us knew how to celebrate.

When we gathered out senses a bit, Vinnie and myself went for a drink down at my mum and dad's pub. A couple of the other lads said they would follow us there. When we were driving along I said to Vinnie that we would be rolling in money if we won the FA Cup and we agreed that, with the money we would make, we would each buy a BMW convertible. Talk about optimistic. What we didn't know was what bonus the club would give us if we won the FA Cup. There was nothing to compare it to because the club had never been involved in a match as big as this before. As it turned out, we picked up about £2,000 for winning the Cup – and we thought we would make about 20 times that. Never mind a BMW – we could just about afford one of its wheels. No one had ever envisaged we would get to the FA Cup final, never mind win it. No one had it in their contracts. But that was still to come. That night we got well and truly drunk because next day the build-up to Wembley started and we knew we would be playing Liverpool.

Chapter 7

the final

The FA Cup final in 1988 was such a huge game for all of us that for the remainder of the league season we were worried sick about getting injured. No one wanted to miss the biggest day of their lives, never mind the most important in Wimbledon's history. Fortunately, we were safe from relegation worries and Bobby Gould was able to rest players from time to time.

The last league game of the season was against Manchester United at Old Trafford. Normally, players would be begging to be involved in a game like that. Not this time. It was about the only time in my life that I was happy to be dropped. In our last training session before the game, Gouldy was handing out the bibs. Then he came up to me and was almost apologetic. 'I am leaving you out at United,' he said. 'Don't get upset – I just want to make sure you're fit for the final.' Upset? I was the most relieved player at the club and I didn't even travel with the squad to Manchester. Vinnie Jones played, though, and it must have been the only game in which he played when he didn't make a tackle. 'I am getting stuck into no one!' said Vinnie, and you could understand his thinking even though it was strange coming from him, one of the hardest men in football. Just for the record we lost 2-1 that day.

With the game at United out of the way, we began the real build-up to Wembley. Between them, Gouldy and Don Howe had come up with a plan to curb John Barnes who they identified as the Liverpool danger man. He was on fire at the time and tearing teams to pieces, as was Peter Beardsley. They were the two we had to stop. I was switched

45

from left wing to right wing to help Clive Goodyear cope with Barnes. I was only young at the time and I could run all day. The message to me was simple: I had to keep showing Barnes away from his left foot. That was his strong one, the one that did the damage. I had to stick to him like a limpet, basically annoy him, make him sick of the sight of me. Beardsley was down to Eric Young and Andy Thorn, our central defenders. Eric was quite quick but Thorny wasn't. Well, his brain was quick but his legs weren't. All week we worked on how to combat them. We worked hour after hour on set pieces to make sure we knew exactly what we would be doing on the big day. With Don Howe, nothing was left to chance.

Technically, we knew they were better players than us but we felt we had more bite, spirit and a greater eagerness to win. They had the players, the names if you like. But Wimbledon had been built on beating reputations and we were determined this would be no different. Everyone in the country expected us to lose and the odds against us were staggering in what was still a two-horse race. You could get 4/1 or 5/1 against us – the longest odds against one team in a cup final, I was told. I never had a bet. I never bet on myself to win but I remember getting the right hump with my uncle who had a big gamble on Liverpool to win 3-0. I told him families should stick together and there he was betting, on us to lose heavily. That did not go down well with me.

The night before the final our preparations were unusual to say the least. We were staying at a hotel in Wimbledon but we just weren't comfortable. They brought in all this posh food and that wasn't for us. It wasn't our style and Bobby Gould knew it.

Myself and Vinnie Jones felt the tension more than most because we were the youngest in the squad and really hyperactive. The whole week had been so different and strange for us. Eric Hall had arranged all this sponsorship and we had to pose for photographs. It all seemed silly at times – we were wearing sunglasses when it was raining and had umbrellas up when the sun was shining.

Gouldy was brilliant. He wanted us comfortable and relaxed so he told us to go down to the town and have some fish and chips. He gave us a few quid and told us to go and have a few beers to unwind. He could see the tension was getting to us and didn't want all our nervous energy used up before Wembley. So we went out, had a bite to eat and a few drinks and were back at the hotel by 11 p.m.

It was no good, though. Neither Vinnie nor myself could sleep so at 6 a.m. we were up and about again. Vinnie suggested we should go down to the town and have a haircut. We also agreed to buy some flowers for Princess Diana, who was presenting the cup. So just after 7 a.m. on cup final morning we jumped into his Fiat Turbo and went into the town. In town we bumped into the actress June Whitfield. June, who is a big Wimbledon supporter, was amazed to see us at that time of the morning. 'Listen,' she said, 'good luck today but go back to the hotel now and get some rest.' The hairdresser couldn't believe it either, not two FA Cup final players coming into his shop that early. He just laughed and wished us all the best. We had the cuts, really short, very severe. Then we had some breakfast and bought some flowers.

When we got back to the hotel, the rest of the lads were getting up for breakfast. Of course me and Vinnie had already had ours. Gouldy spotted us and called us over. The three of us went for a walk. He knew we had gone out because he'd noticed that Vinnie's car was missing. He also knew how excited we were. 'Go over there,' he said, pointing at a bench in the gardens of the hotel grounds, 'and rest. Or go back to your room and have a sleep. Whatever you do, calm down. We will need everything you have at 3 o'clock and the rate you two are going you won't have anything left.' So we sat on this veranda overlooking the hotel patio. We started to wind down. One disappointment was that we were told we wouldn't be allowed to present Princess Diana with the flowers. That was a pity.

Then stories began to emerge about other players and one involved Terry Gibson. Gouldy had gone to his room at around 8.30 a.m. to see if all was alright. Gibbo came to the door still half-asleep and stark naked . . . except for a brand new pair of football boots. He had been given some by sponsors and wore them in bed all night to help break them in so they felt comfortable during the game. Gouldy just cracked up at the sight in front of him. He couldn't tell the story for laughing and I must admit I couldn't imagine a Liverpool player walking about like that at 8.30 a.m. on cup final day.

On the coach to the ground we started playing cards. It was a glorious May day. I had never known the chaps so relaxed. There was no pressure on us. People were talking about Liverpool beating Wimbledon and winning by a record score. But we were the underdogs and we knew that outside Merseyside, everyone wanted us to win. The papers were full of articles about the two sets of players, comparing their earnings and how much they would collect if they won the FA Cup. By then we all knew it would be just over £2,000 for us, and Vinnie and myself started joking about the BMWs we weren't going to buy.

Then I appeared on television. When I was fourteen I had played in a team that won an under-15 five-a-side competition at Wembley arena and later that year I was invited on *Record Breakers* with the late Roy Castle. Myself and a lad called Philip Bowles – he scored a hat-trick in the final – were in the studio doing tricks and kicking a ball between ourselves and then we were interviewed by Roy Castle. He talked to Philip about his hat-trick and then asked me what I wanted to do. I said I wanted to be a professional footballer and that I wanted to play in the FA Cup final and pick up the FA Cup. Yes, I knew what I wanted to do at 14. Anyway they played a tape of that interview on the Wimbledon coach on the way to Wembley that day and, when you think about it, it was such a prophetic thing to come up with – especially when you look at what happened between then and when I eventually signed professional with Wimbledon.

Then the cameras switched to us on the coach live. 'What are you doing?' I was asked and, as soon as I started to talk, Vinnie grabbed hold of me between the legs and squeezed really hard. It really did hurt! 'I am losing my money at cards at the moment,' I answered and, as they switched to Vinnie, I grabbed hold of him in the same way and really squeezed hard. We were both trying to carry on as though nothing was happening. Then, when the rest of the lads saw the film of me at the age of 14, I got bombarded with all kinds of rubbish. But that summed up the mood that morning. We were so at ease it was untrue.

When we got to Wembley and saw inside the stadium itself, it was amazing. It took your breath away. No one had ever seen anything like it. Bobby Gould and Don Howe knew what to expect but we certainly didn't as players. The dressing rooms were something else. It was like staying at a five-star hotel. They were stunning. We had never seen such luxury. I am sure that gave us a lift. Liverpool were a team full of internationals. They had all been to Wembley before. It was nothing new to them. For us it was one great adventure. But rather than feel intimidated by the surroundings, they gave us a tremendous boost. We felt important. Raggy-arsed Wimbledon were at Wembley and we were going to make the most of it.

When we walked out on to the pitch for the pre-match walkabout, the stadium was really filling up and we had an idea of what we were up against in terms of support. When you looked at the colours all round the stadium, well, we might as well have been playing at Anfield. The whole place was like a sea of red and white. Yes, we had our allocation of 20,000 or so tickets and you could see the blue and yellow scarves. But it was predominantly red and white. Put off? You must be joking. Wimbledon love that kind of situation. And we were used to it. We just went out to soak it all up. It was lovely. I remember talking to Vinnie Jones as we were walking around and he had one plan in his mind. 'If I get the chance, I am going to sort them out, leave my mark,' he said. 'I want to let them know it's not going to be easy for them. I want them to know this is going to be a hard day. In a fight you have to take out the leader.' And if you recall, he did just that with his early tackle on Steve McMahon. It was his way of letting their 'leader' know we weren't afraid of them. I was saying to him before we went out that he was important to us, that he would have to make his point for the rest of us. 'Don't worry about it Ratso,' he said. 'Leave it to me.'

The whole atmosphere really inspired me, not by making me

nervous or anything, I just wanted to get out there and play. I couldn't wait for kick-off.

There was a bit of a sad moment when Gouldy named the team and the substitutes. Brian Gayle had been a big part of what we had achieved as a club but Gouldy had said that, if people got themselves sent off and the man who came in did well, that could cost them their place in the FA Cup team. Gayle had been sent off in the sixth round against Watford and was left out of the semi-final. As it turned out, he missed the final as well. He was almost crying when his place on the subs' bench went to Laurie Cunningham and we really felt for him. But when that was over, it was clear that as a team we were really fired up.

Then we were in the tunnel. I had no idea what it's usually like down there, whether you are supposed to be quiet and well-mannered, but we weren't going to change our pre-match routine. 'Yidaho' came the shout down the tunnel as we lined up. It was John Fashanu. He always shouted that before we went out. It was like a battle cry. It wasn't to put Liverpool under pressure or anything like that. I mean, look at all the internationals in their team and the big games they had played. They weren't going to be put off by a Wimbledon player shouting down the tunnel at Wembley. Fash would say it as much to wind himself up and the feeling spread to the rest of the players. Liverpool? They came out all calm and relaxed. They had seen it and done it all before. But I think deep down inside they knew that, as we had done well against them in the past, we could give them problems that day. The noise at Wembley on FA Cup final day is incredible. It is like hitting a wall. You have to steady yourself and really concentrate or you can get badly affected.

All in all, the pressure really was on them, not us. We were the no-hopers and they were the superstars. The whole nation expected them to win. They may have wanted us to win as the underdogs but logic said that Liverpool would beat us. They were household names, we were nobodies. But that can bring its own problems. We were relaxed about it all. We just wanted to get on with the game. Liverpool HAD to win. I mean, who wanted to be the team beaten by the biggest underdogs in the history of FA Cup finals?

The game was Liverpool's at the start and there was a crucial point in the first half. Peter Beardsley had broken through and was fouled by Andy Thorn. It looked as though he was going to fall over and lose the ball and the referee blew for a free-kick. But Beardsley somehow kept his balance and went on to score. To be fair Dave Beasant had heard the whistle and made no attempt to save the shot. But the ball was brought back for the foul. Liverpool went potty and just moaned and moaned. They thought the referee Brian Hill should have played advantage and allowed Beardsley to carry on. But these things have a habit of evening themselves out and Liverpool got their own back in the second half with a penalty that was dubious to say the least. But that was still to come.

Soon after the Beardsley 'goal', we were given a free-kick down on the left wing. And that is when Lawrie Sanchez made history for Wimbledon – by mistake! He shouldn't have been in that place to head the ball home. It should have been Alan Cork. The plan was for me to drill the ball over really hard, as if I was having a shot at goal. Then Corky was supposed to jump up and head it in. But Corky, a really good header of the ball, stayed out of the space for some reason and Sanchez went there. And Sanchez got the touch. In it went and we just couldn't believe it. The seconds afterwards are just a blur. We went wild. I ran up and jumped on Sanchez with my body covering his face. He always gives me grief about that. You know, the biggest moment of his life and in every picture his face is covered. 'I scored the winning goal in the cup final and all people see is your face and my body,' he kept moaning. I always say that I did it on purpose because so many kids would see that picture of his face it would give them nightmares.

About ten minutes later, the whistle went for half-time. We got into the dressing room in a state of disbelief. Wimbledon leading Liverpool. That was in no one's script. We sat there and it was clear the heat was taking its toll. That is when we saw Don Howe at his best. Seeing how hot it was before the game he told our kit-man Sid Fish – I reckon he has been at Wimbledon forever and the consensus of opinion is that he must be about two days younger than God! – to make sure we had lots of towels soaked in cold water ready for us when we came in. To make sure he had them ready for us, Sid must have left after about 25 minutes of the game. 'Shirts off, get your shorts off,' shouted Don when we came in. 'Now put these on. Quick.' What with the temperature on the day, the excitement of the occasion and the fact we were leading 1-0, every one of us was hyper. The towel ploy really worked. Suddenly we all calmed down and relaxed. We were able to start focusing on the second half. The tension and the heat just went and that showed the benefits of having an experienced man like Don as part of the set-up. He was invaluable that day.

We talked about our strategy for the second half. To be honest neither Gouldy nor Don Howe expected us to be in front. They were as excited as us at first. Then we made our resolution for the second 45 minutes – defend for our lives. For a long while it worked. They just couldn't break us down – but then the referee gave them a lifeline. The ball was played into our penalty area and John Aldridge ran on to it. Clive Goodyear made his challenge and got his toe to the ball to prod it back to Dave Beasant. No problem – or so we thought. We couldn't believe it when the referee pointed to the spot. This is it, I thought, this is our payback for that Peter Beardsley incident in the first half. There was no way in the world that it was a penalty. I thought that was our FA Cup chance gone because I couldn't see us scoring again, not in a million years, unless we got lucky from a set piece. That was the only time we were giving them any kind of problem. We had done so well and now it was going to count for nothing. But I had underestimated Dave Beasant. He has always been very thorough and I should have known he would have genned up on what any Liverpool penalty taker – usually John Aldridge – would do. He had, and he pulled off a tremendous save.

Then I was so out of order. I ran up to Aldridge and really gloried in his miss. I shouldn't have done it and I know that but I had seen him taking the mickey out of people who had made mistakes in the past and, as much as I was doing it for me and Wimbledon, I was doing it for all of them. I saw him, a few years later, go up and ruffle the hair of Brian Laws of Nottingham Forest when he scored an own-goal against Liverpool. I didn't like that attitude, so I really rubbed it in when Dave Beasant saved his spot-kick.

After that, they really had only one more chance, when Dave Beasant flapped at a corner, but there was never a problem. We held on to cause the biggest upset in an FA Cup final ever. Little Wimbledon had beaten mighty Liverpool, the champions. And didn't we milk the moment. Their fans looked really low and so did their players. I can recall Alan Hansen looking really, really down. I mean, it is not the sort of thing you want on your CV, is it, getting beaten by Wimbledon? To be honest, though, I don't even recall shaking hands with their players. We didn't bother with them or how they felt. We just got together in a huge party. We were determined just to lap it all up, every moment, every second.

Then we went up to collect the trophy. It was a brilliant feeling walking up those steps as winners and it is everything that anyone who has done it tells you it is. You are exhausted, you are knackered, but you feel as if you're floating. Perhaps it was the exhaustion but I proceeded to make a real idiot of myself in front of Princess Diana. Dave Beasant went first and took the cup and I took the top. I put it on my head. Just then, I heard a voice. It was a mate of mine who was shouting 'Wisey, Wisey' and clenching his fists. I saw him and shouted back 'You bastard'. Apparently what I said was clearly heard on television and Princess Diana was standing right behind me. But she just smiled. She knew I was young and excited and that this was a great moment for me. But some members of the public weren't so under-standing. The club had dozens of letters of complaint about it. I didn't mean any harm or disrespect. It was the excitement of the moment that got to me.

Back down on the pitch, Gouldy started going on about enjoying it all. He called us together and said to take everything in, not miss a minute or a second of a great day. 'This might never happen to you again; enjoy it all.' And with that Vinnie gave a typical response. He grabbed him between the legs. 'Just shut up!' we said and carried on with our celebrations round the pitch. We walked slow, really slow, savouring every second. We were not going to miss an instant. As we went round, the Liverpool fans who had stayed behind clapped us and I thought that was a great gesture.

When we reached the part of the pitch underneath the television gantry, Gouldy stopped to look up at Dave Bassett. He was there as part of a commentary team. Gouldy then took the FA Cup and pointed at it. 'This is yours, Harry,' he shouted and that was a fantastic thing to do. It was Gouldy's way of saying that the progress made by the club was down to Harry and that it should not be forgotten. He didn't need to do that but he knew how pleased Harry would have been for us and that this achievement was as much Harry's as anyone's. Although Gouldy had told us to just stay out and take it all in, the truth was we couldn't wait to get back down to the dressing room to start the party among ourselves. On reflection, we should have stayed out there longer.

I have to be honest and say that the celebrations that night were a blur. A complete blur. I can recall going back to Plough Lane on the coach after we picked up our things from the hotel, and I remember going on television the following morning, but I don't remember much in between. We had a post-match knees-up at Plough Lane, and I do know that it was that night that I really got to know Eric Hall. Fash had brought him in to organise the players' pool to divvy up all the money that we had made from interviews and stuff. He had organised everything really well. I liked him straight away. He is a genuinely funny man who never stops talking and keeps using his 'Monster, Monster' catchphrase. Typical Eric, he had a real flamboyant sense of dress and was wearing a bright yellow shirt and puffing on this huge cigar. Right beside him, as always, was his mobile phone. He asked me if I wanted him to be my agent and I just asked what I had to do. 'Nothing,' he said. 'That's my job, I do everything.' He told me I didn't have to sign anything. He said a handshake was enough and that on the strength of that he would look after my interests from then on. 'And if you want to walk away, then you can do at any time,' he added. 'There will be nothing on paper.' That sounded good to me. If there were going to be any problems working with Eric, I didn't want any long, legal aggravation to release me from any contract. I agreed, and a few hours later he had me working. We must have stayed at Plough Lane until about 4 a.m. and it seemed like I had been in bed five minutes when Eric told me he had arranged his first job – a television interview with me and Dave Beasant at 7 a.m. To this day, I can't recall a thing about what was said or done in that interview. All I wanted to do was go back to bed. But Eric showed that he wasted no time and that was alright by me.

Eric is a controversial character. A lot of people who have dealings with him trust him about as far as they can throw him. But I know one thing about him for sure – I would trust him with my life. He is totally loyal to his clients. If he doesn't work for you, quite simply he doesn't care about you. His commitment is to those people on his books. He works with a simple philosophy: 'I try to make poor players rich and rich players richer'. He knows nothing about football and he makes a joke about that. 'I would ban the free-kick on principle,' he has always said.

All he wants is to earn you money. The more you get, the more he gets. But he won't have you doing things just for the sake of it. He is not as mercenary as people think. Very frequently he will turn down work on my behalf because he doesn't think it is in my interests. That is not true of all agents and, when I look at some of them about nowadays, I wouldn't touch them with a bargepole. I trust Eric and, if he wasn't good at his job, then I wouldn't be with him. If he didn't do well for me, I wouldn't have him as my agent. He has looked after me for more than ten years, so that must tell you something. In that time I haven't signed one piece of paper, so I could walk away tomorrow. But I won't.

He has now become a good friend of mine and I trust him like a brother. We talk and he gives me honest advice. He could have me working every day but he knows that would be detrimental to my career as a player. No, he is very selective about what he has me doing, and, although he is a workaholic, he makes sure that nothing gets in the way of my playing. He knows when to speak and when not to speak – for instance, he will never ring me the night before a game or the morning of a game. His background is in the world of show business and probably from working in that world he has tremendous front. I have been sitting there when he has been negotiating my contracts and sometimes I can't believe the things he asks for to get me a better deal. But he gets the job done. Not so long ago, he was very ill with food poisoning and I thought he was going to die. I was so upset and just prayed for him to recover. Thankfully, he did. And now he is back to his normal self.

For me there has never been a day like that FA Cup final, before or since. The only things that have ever run it close were the cup wins with Chelsea at Wembley and in Europe. It was amazing how my world had been turned upside-down in just over three years. Then, I was too ashamed to sign on the dole. Now I was an FA Cup winner after beating one of the biggest clubs in Europe.

Chapter 8

after wembley

That summer the inevitable happened. The Crazy Gang broke up. Other clubs wanted to instil the Wimbledon spirit into their own teams and the offers started to come in for us. The club owner Sam Hammam had invited them really. When he was asked straight after the FA Cup final how many players he would sell, he said, 'All of them, at a price.' He knew the club, with its crowds and limited resources, had to cash in on the success. There was to be little more income through winning the trophy because, at the time, English clubs were banned from European football, so there was to be no revenue from playing in the Cup Winners' Cup. Many of the players who helped win the FA Cup wanted to go during the summer – and I was one of them. I was desperate in fact. I wanted to further my career, maybe earn a bit more money.

Sam Hammam said I could go if someone bid £1 million. Eric Hall objected and said that price-tag wasn't reflected in my wages which were about £300 a week at the time. Eric told me that both Arsenal and Spurs were interested and that Terry Venables – who was in charge at White Hart Lane at the time – was particularly keen. But Wimbledon turned down any inquiry about me that would pay less than £1 million and I was steaming about it. I felt they weren't paying me enough to stay there and, anyway, I felt I had done all I could for Wimbledon. It was time for me to move. Andy Thorn and Dave Beasant had gone to Newcastle and I wanted a new start too.

But Bobby Gould and Sam Hammam were having none of it. I was staying and that was that. I was livid . . . so livid that I decided not to turn up for the pre-season tour to Sweden. I said I had a bad back and couldn't travel or play. Eventually I did go along but I proceeded to cause havoc – by letting off fireworks in the hotel corridor. I wanted to do everything possible to make them put me up for sale. I wanted them to be sick of me. I was late for team meetings and generally disruptive. All Bobby Gould did was smile. He refused to let me get the better of him and just didn't react no matter what I did. Contrast that to what he did with Roger Joseph, one of our defenders. He turned up late just once or twice for team meetings – and was sent home. I was letting off fireworks, always late and yet he never said a thing.

It was really getting to me. I was disgusted with Sam Hammam. He just wouldn't budge and neither would Gouldy. When we came back from Sweden I took in a transfer request EVERY day. Bobby Gould would just laugh every time I came in and in the end wouldn't even read them. He just threw them in the bin in his office. Finally, he said he wanted to talk about a new contract. I spoke with Eric Hall about it and he said I might as well sign because in a year's time I could be on my way if a big enough offer came in that Wimbledon would find hard to reject. So I signed for an extra year and my pay went up to £70,000 a year. But Gouldy knew I wasn't happy and, although I was on a lot more money, my last two years at Wimbledon weren't enjoyable ones.

I got myself into some bother outside the club too. It was what turned out to be my last night out with the Wimbledon lads – and I ended up losing my driving licence. I was stupid, very stupid. But when you are young you do stupid things, and I paid the price and learned my lesson about drinking and driving. In those days, there wasn't the stigma to that kind of offence that there is now but that is no excuse. I shouldn't have done it.

It started after the last game of the season and Sam Hammam had booked a night out for us at a restaurant called Joe Allen's. We had all had a few drinks there and Sam had arranged for us to go on to a club called Madame Jo-Jo's in Soho, which is famous for its drag acts. Sam had said it was something we had to see and, although we weren't too keen at the start of the evening, as the drinks went down we were more and more agreeable, saying it would be a great laugh.

Anyway, we were driving along Piccadilly in my car and I was with my good friend and team-mate Vaughan Ryan. Next to us at the lights was John Scales in his car. It was pouring with rain. Suddenly Scalesy jumped out and shouted we should have a race. I agreed – and he promptly pulled up my windscreen wipers. That gave him a head start, as I had to get out to put them back. Vaughan said he knew a short cut and directed me down a side street. I turned straight down it not noticing the No Entry sign, or the policeman in the street. He pulled me over, asked for the keys and told me to step out. The problem was I then got my foot stuck in the seatbelt and tripped over on to the road. Vaughan cracked up, the policeman didn't. He asked if I had been drinking and I said one or two. He then asked me to blow into a breathalyser and I refused. He asked again and I refused. Then he said I was under arrest and called for a van to take me to the police station. Then I decided I wanted to blow into the bag, but he said no, he had asked me twice, I had refused and now I was arrested. I asked if Vaughan could follow the van in the car and he agreed – without knowing Vaughan was just as drunk as me.

At the station, I was asked to blow into a bag once more and I messed it up. I was then charged with failing to provide a specimen. Eventually, I was banned for a year and fined. I learned a huge lesson from that. I went out that night thinking that as a young player with a few quid in my pocket, I could get away with anything. You just don't think at that age, you just don't worry. I do now and I never drink and drive these days.

But it wasn't all bad that summer. I was called up to the England squad and then I got the phone call from Bobby Gould that I had been waiting for. I was at my mum's when he rang to say that Wimbledon had accepted a £1.6 million bid for me from Chelsea. 'Do you want to go?' he asked, knowing full well what my answer was going to be. 'Too bleedin' right I do.' He laughed, because he knew I was desperate to find another club. He wished me all the best and told me to enjoy myself.

The arrangement was that I was to go to Stamford Bridge with Eric Hall to meet the Chelsea manager, Bobby Campbell, and the chairman, Ken Bates. The day before I went, they had signed Andy Townsend from Norwich and apparently he looked immaculate when he turned up in a suit and tie. Me? I just wore a tracksuit. I just hadn't a clue what to wear. Ken Bates took one look at me and said, 'I see you are dressed for the occasion.' I just said, 'Hello Batesy, how are you?' You know, I think he liked my cheek. I was just natural with him and he replied, 'Who are you calling Batesy?' But he was smiling when he said it.

The talks didn't take long at all and everything was agreed – but then there was a phone call from Sam Hammam that could have wrecked it. I was told Sam was on the line and wanted to speak to me urgently. 'You can't sign yet,' he said. 'It has not all been sorted out.' He said he was coming straight down to Stamford Bridge. A little later I saw him and Eric outside the offices where I had been with Bobby Campbell and Ken Bates. 'You know Dennis, it hurts me that you have to go,' he said. 'You are one of the family. But Dennis, you know we have not got a lot of money at Wimbledon and that we owe you £35,000. So, if you want to go, you have to sign this paper to say you will forfeit the money because you asked for a transfer.'

That money was part of the signing-on fee I was due. You lose it if you ask for a move but I hadn't asked to leave since I agreed the new deal. I was gobsmacked. I was entitled to that money but Sam wouldn't budge: I had to sign a piece of paper to say that I had asked for a move and that would mean no £35,000. I was really upset. How could Wimbledon say they didn't have any money? I cost them nothing and yet I was being sold for £1.6 million and here was Sam saying he couldn't afford £35,000. Eric encouraged me to hold out, saying that I would get my money; they had to pay me. But I said no, I wasn't going to take that chance. After trying so hard for so long to get my transfer, I was quite willing to give up what was owed to me. I was determined the move would go through and was not going to let Sam Hammam spoil it for me. So I signed the bit of paper which said I had asked for a move.

When we got back into the office, Ken Bates asked what all the fuss had been about. Eric Hall explained what had gone on and that I had signed what was tantamount to a transfer request and with it signed away £35,000. Batesy looked astonished. 'What?' he said. 'He has given up £35,000 just to come to this club?' He immediately got in touch with the managing director Colin Hutchinson and had an extra £35,000 put on my contract at Chelsea. From that day, Ken Bates and myself have always got on. He was impressed with how much I wanted to join Chelsea and I was impressed with the way he made a gesture he had no obligation to do.

Chapter 9

chelsea football club

Chelsea have always had the image and the reputation of a big club. At one time they were known as the glamour club of London. But since the early seventies they had the problem of being the perennial under-achievers of London football. I hoped to play my part in changing that when I joined in July 1990 but I could see from the start what a huge job was required. The potential was there alright but potential does not satisfy supporters or ambitious players. They never won anything; it was as simple as that. A cup run was always a possibility but it wasn't until the arrival of Glenn Hoddle that the profile of the club changed again.

Time and patience were needed but eventually Ken Bates got it right. For a start the stadium needed a complete re-vamp. Before, it was like one of those huge concrete bowls of a stadium that you still see in Eastern Europe, not at all intimidating, not to the smaller clubs anyway. For the glamour teams there wasn't too much of a problem either. We had a good record against them because we invariably played in front of a full house and even at the old Stamford Bridge, that created an atmosphere. But play Southampton on a Wednesday night in February and only 11,000 were turning up and there was nothing to scare them. Now it is different. The stadium is magnificent. The crowd are much closer to the pitch and they can intimidate anyone . . . which is exactly how it should be if home advantage is going to count for anything.

With the team we have and the football we are playing now, there are full houses for most games and no one likes playing there. It has all come good and Batesy must take much of the credit. He was patient and now the rewards are coming. You only have to look at what Manchester United have achieved over the last six or seven years to see the benefit of patience. That is what I want Chelsea to be doing: winning league titles and European competitions. But you have to get the foundations right and money doesn't guarantee that. Just look at Blackburn and the money they have spent. Yes, they won a league title a few years back but now they are back in the First Division. I want to be part of a club that is making progress, not going backwards, and at last I feel I am part of such a club at Chelsea. Trophies are coming in now and the next target is the Premiership. The squad we have now is not just for this season – it is for the future.

I joined a Chelsea team that had just been promoted to the old First Division and they already had some quality players – Kerry Dixon, Erland Johnsen, Graham Roberts, Steve Clarke, Gordon Durie, Graeme Le Saux and, of course, Andy Townsend. But it was a funny atmosphere down there. Andy and myself weren't quite sure what was going on. There seemed to be cliques; players seemed to have their own little groups.

I was the record signing for Chelsea at the time and that made me feel a bit awkward. I felt people look at me and maybe doubt my abilities. In fact Kerry Dixon was the only one who came over to me and said, 'Am I glad you're here. Now I'll get some decent crosses and score some goals.' He made me very welcome and we were often room-mates while we were at the club together. But I couldn't get over the little groups. It was something I wasn't used to after Wimbledon. This was different and I was uncomfortable with it. Kevin McAllister, Steve Clarke and Gordon Durie were one group, Kenneth Monkou, Erland Johnsen and Graeme Le Saux were in another. Then there was Graham Roberts who was having his problems with the club for one reason or another and wanted to leave. It was hard to get used to, especially after the Wimbledon atmosphere.

I played well in my first game, though. It was against Derby and we won 2-1. Dave Beasant had joined the club the previous season and it was a relief for me that he was there. At least one face was familiar. Bes was a hero in that game, saving a penalty. Who says lightning never strikes twice?

But in my third game it all went a bit wrong for me. We were at Crystal Palace, who had players like Mark Bright, Ian Wright and Andy Gray in the team. There was a bit of an atmosphere down there and everyone was a bit hyped up and from the start, the tackles were flying. But the last thing I expected was to get sent off after just nine minutes. Myself and Andy Gray went for a 50-50 ball. We got up and started having a push and shove at each other, no punches or anything like that. But the referee saw it differently – and showed us both the red card. When I got to the tunnel, Andy Gray was waiting there and there was another scrap. Eventually, the assistant manager Gwyn Williams got me into the dressing room, told me to get changed and advised me to go straight home. There were going to be a lot of press waiting for me after the game and he thought it was better I went home. All of which left my parents more than puzzled. They were delayed on their way to the game and arrived 20 minutes late. I was almost home before they sat down. When they looked on the pitch, they couldn't see me so they asked the people next to them where I was. Had I been injured in the warm-up or something? They couldn't believe it when they were told I had been sent off.

That incident brought it home to me just what being at a big club was all about. I mean, that kind of thing seemed to happen every week at Wimbledon and no one made a fuss. You could do things down there and get away with it. This was Chelsea and this was different. I cost a lot of money and things like a disciplinary record did matter. You are put under the microscope all the time and you have to curb your temper. After the match Bobby Campbell was asked about my chances of playing for England, whether I had the right temperament and stuff like that. But Bobby told me that he didn't want me to change. He knew I was a competitive player who hated losing, be it a game or a tackle. That is why he spent so much money on me. But I have to say all the fuss and furore did get to me and my form suffered. Suddenly, after a decent start, I wasn't playing all that well.

As far as all the talk about me not having the right temperament to play international football was concerned, well all I can say is that the new England manager Graham Taylor didn't listen to it. I was picked for a European Championship qualifier over in Turkey. Mind you, I was only in the squad for a couple of games and then discarded. I was never given a reason. Obviously he didn't fancy me any more. But I made my debut against Turkey in 1990 and I was both proud and delighted – especially as I scored the winning goal. It was a vital win in our group because that night the Republic of Ireland drew 0-0 at home to Poland and dropped two vital points.

The assistant manager of England at the time was Lawrie McMenemy. It was the first time I had seen him since I left Southampton. But there was never a problem between us as far as England was concerned. In fact, when I joined up he was very apologetic about what had happened before, and he was always very nice to me whenever I was with England. He could have gone the other way in view of our history and I suppose he could have argued against Graham Taylor picking me and tried to get me left out. But clearly he didn't and that shows he was a big man and I have always had a lot of respect for him because of that. Even though he had long left Southampton and I was now a Chelsea player I still called him gaffer. I certainly held no grudge and, when you look at it, he really did me a favour by letting me go. I really don't know if I would have done that well at Southampton had I stayed.

The goal I scored was more than a bit lucky. The ball hit me after Gary Pallister headed on a Stuart Pearce free-kick, and it went in. After the game Lawrie didn't want me saying too much to the press and told me not to be too concerned about it being a streaky goal. 'It won't show that in the record books,' he said. 'It will just show your name. It doesn't matter how you score.'

I was involved in the next match against Russia at Wembley and at the end of the 1990-91 season went on the tour to the Far East, Australia and New Zealand. I came on as substitute against Australia and played twice against New Zealand. I was also called up by England to be part of the squad for the Rous Cup matches in 1989 against Chile at Wembley and against Scotland in Glasgow. I was substitute against Chile but not involved against the Scots. But I was very much involved in a card school with Chris Woods, Peter Shilton and Tony Cottee, and I fleeced them. Peter Shilton started off by looking after me when we were with the England squad. He knew it was awkward for me because I was new to the international scene and he was like a protector. He remembered me from the days at Southampton when I used to clean his boots – but he also remembered me for something else when he paid me my card school money . . . all £460 of it. I was so proud that I asked him to sign a £10 note for me and he wrote, 'To Dennis, lucky sod – Peter Shilton'. I still have that note in my scrapbook.

At Chelsea, though, it was a strange first season – yet another one of under-achievement at Stamford Bridge. We were one of the teams tipped to do well and we certainly had the players there. But somehow we just didn't gel. The dressing room had a funny atmosphere and at the time the club were trying to get rid of a few players. Gordon Durie, Kevin McAllister and Steve Clarke were not too friendly towards me. Maybe it was because they thought I had been brought in to replace McAllister. What I do know is that, when the other two left, Clarkey became a better person and to this day he is a very good friend of mine. But he wasn't saying much to me at the time. I did make a good pal in Kevin Hitchcock, though. Once we cleared the air over the business at Mansfield, we got on really well.

Maybe it was the fee and trying to justify it, maybe it was because I had come from Wimbledon, but I just didn't feel at ease at Chelsea that first season. The punters liked me because of the way I played. Fans always warm to players who give everything for the club and they could see I was trying my heart out. But still I felt the pressure, more on me than Andy Townsend, because I was the record signing. I always felt I had to justify it. Andy was playing magnificently but my form wasn't that great. I always felt I was being looked at differently because of the fee and it was so unlike what I had been used to at Wimbledon. I can't tell you how relieved I was the following summer when we bought Robert Fleck from Norwich for £2.1 million. That made him the record buy and took the pressure off me. He felt the same as me for a long time and, believe me, it is hard to be comfortable with that burden of expectancy, especially when you're young.

All round Chelsea, I just felt it wasn't quite right. The pitch wasn't good and the stadium wasn't good. Everything needed sorting out. That wasn't the fault of Ken Bates. He was doing his best on all fronts. At the time he was fighting to keep the club going from the threat of Stamford Bridge being developed. He put what money he could into the team, like the £3 million sponsorship from Commodore, which was spent buying me and Andy Townsend. I think he knew that we were short of what was needed to win the league and he would have been happy with one of the cups while he sorted things out financially. He knew what he wanted to do but he also knew it would take time. That wasn't much good to the fans, though, and at times they were really fed up. And you could hear it as well. They knew Chelsea were a big club and were the original sleeping giants. Eventually we woke up but that was a lot later on.

Bobby Campbell was the manager who signed me but I can't honestly say I got on well with him. I didn't really like him and I certainly didn't like the way he treated certain players. For me, he ruined the career of Alan Dickens, a midfield player we had signed from West Ham. On the training pitch he was forever shouting at him, sometimes screaming. I remember he stopped one session and shouted really loud, 'Are you ever going to talk?' Alan was a very talented lad with a lot of ability. But he was also very quiet and reserved. He wasn't right from that day, his confidence had gone. He had been destroyed in front of the rest of the squad and he never recovered from it.

That was typical of Campbell. He used to choose which players to have a go at . . . usually the quiet ones. He made an example of them, in training or after a game. But he wouldn't do it to the older ones. It was also annoying how he kept mentioning Liverpool. It was Liverpool this, Liverpool that. Everything was how great Liverpool were and no one is happy hearing that all the time. I found him a bit arrogant as well – and a bit flash. The lads used to crack up at the way he used to keep flicking his Rolex watch around so that everyone would notice it.

He was very full of himself and I don't know too many players who got on well with him. In particular, they didn't like reading about what was going to happen with the team selection from the news-papers. There was one time when things weren't going well and we were playing Manchester United at Old Trafford in a televised game. All the headlines were about how he was going to leave out the 'Four Ds' and play the kids instead. Gordon Durie, Kerry Dixon, Dennis Wise and Tony Dorigo weren't too impressed to read that. He changed his mind at the last minute and we won 3-2. But the threat, as I saw it, was to show everyone how strong he was. It was just as well that he didn't go through with it because he would have lost an awful lot of respect from the players if he had. Players don't like reading things like that. He did it to me once and I had a right go at him about it. I read I was going to be dropped before he told me and there is nothing worse than that. I much preferred the Harry Bassett approach – 'because you were crap last week'. A least it was to your face. But Campbell wasn't straight down the line.

Our biggest achievement that season was to reach the semi-finals of the Rumbelows Cup, but again we flopped when we were in sight of a major honour. It was over two legs and we lost 2-0 at home and 3-1 away at Sheffield Wednesday. It was another shambles of a season. I admit I was more than a little depressed although it was a good education for me. You always assume that the grass is greener on the other side and I knew then that wasn't the case. I recall when Wimbledon came to Stamford Bridge and I was left out of the team. Bobby Gould saw me and he could see I was really down. He told me to keep plugging away, to keep going and it would come right. Eventually it did but not for some time. Then there was the league game against Wimbledon away. I was the £1.6 million player against a full-back called Gary Elkins who they had signed for £35,000 from Fulham. Of course, the press built up the game as a contest between the two of us. I had a nightmare and he played well. We lost 2-1 and did I get some stick. It sort of summed up the season for me, and for the team come to that. We had some great results too, like a 6-4 win over Derby, but we also lost 7-0 at Nottingham Forest. (Thankfully, I didn't play in that game.) Basically, it didn't go well under Campbell. He had spent a fair bit of money on players but they just didn't click. We weren't united and you have to be if you are going to be successful. Wimbledon didn't have anywhere near the quality that Chelsea had but there was unity and, with that, strength and spirit.

The vibes were not good at Stamford Bridge. But not once did I regret the move. I knew I had to leave Wimbledon to better myself and in that first season I did get to play for my country. Yes, the atmosphere was bad but not once did I say, even to myself, I shouldn't have come to Chelsea. It wasn't as cosy and wonderful as I thought it would be at a big club but that is maybe no bad thing. It motivates you more to be a success. I remember the first impression I had of Chelsea. I saw that when you went in the main foyer at Stamford Bridge there were lifts. I thought to myself at the time that this must be some set-up. Lifts? At Wimbledon there were only a few staircases.

But then I realised it wasn't in many ways a lot different from what I had left. The training ground was at Harlington, a big open, cold space where the wind always seemed to be blowing. Just like Wimbledon. The dressing rooms were not great. Just like Wimbledon. And we had finished mid-table. But while that might be acceptable at Wimbledon, it wasn't at Chelsea with their status, history and huge support. It was a disappointing season and Bobby Campbell paid the price when he was replaced in May 1991.

Chapter 10

two managers

Bobby Campbell left before the start of the 1991-92 season. They didn't say he was sacked, it was put much nicer than that – he had been 'moved upstairs'. Ian Porterfield was to be the next manager and I can recall the rest of the lads saying he would be great for us. He had worked at the club before and they really liked him.

I was happier and more settled at the end of the summer of 1991. I felt that I was gaining the respect of the others after that first season. When I met Porters for the first time, I really liked him. What the other lads had said was true: he was a great bloke, but in many ways he was too nice to be a manager. He made a great appointment when he made Don Howe his assistant. I knew from my days at Wimbledon that he was one of the best coaches around. He was very shrewd tactically and I really welcomed him coming to the club. He brought in a sense of discipline and that is vital. He gave us a hard pre-season and we looked a leaner, sharper unit all-round. But just before Christmas, he fell seriously ill and couldn't work with us any more. I can't tell you how much we missed him. He kept everyone on their toes and refused to let standards slip. He was just what we wanted and needed and his loss was a huge blow to us.

While he was working with us we were up there in fifth or sixth place but after he left we lost our way and that was very disappointing. We felt that as a team and as a unit we were going places, making real progress. Since I arrived at the club, we had had the team of the 1970s shoved down our throats. We so much wanted to achieve something for ourselves, on our own, to get our own place in the history of Chelsea Football Club. When we lost Don Howe, our hopes for that season went with him.

Thankfully he made a complete recovery and no one was happier about that than me. But it wasn't the same without him. Ian Porterfield brought in Stan Ternent to replace Don Howe and he was a nice feller. The problem was that we now had two nice blokes in charge of the team and, with the strong characters we had on the playing staff at the time, the discipline went more than a bit. Basically, people did what they wanted – and they got away with it. Don Howe had kept us on our toes but that kind of edge had gone now.

After he'd been there a few weeks, Porters asked me about what it would be like to have Vinnie Jones at the club and I said that I thought he would be great for us. I reckoned he would liven the place up – and he did. It was great for me to have Vinnie there. He joined in August 1991 and we were back as a partnership.

The way things were going that season, I thought we could do well in the FA Cup. The league – as it always seemed to – had slipped away but we had reached the sixth round of the cup and had a home draw with Sunderland. You have to fancy your chances when you reach that stage of the competition against a team like Sunderland. This, we felt, was our year, we were going to make our mark. All was going to plan when we went 1-0 up through Clive Allen. The semi-finals were in sight. Then, with not long to go, it was typical Chelsea again, we gave away a really crap goal when John Byrne equalised. That meant a replay at Roker Park and, although we were disappointed not to have won first time, we still knew we had a chance in the replay. Away teams have a good record in the sixth round, probably because the expectation is so high and the pressure is so great.

Anyway, during the second half we were holding them 1-1 (I scored our goal after Peter Davenport put them ahead) and we were looking not bad. Then came the goal which summed up our season. The ball was played towards our goal and Dave Beasant was favourite to get it. But Frank Sinclair didn't hear a call, if there was one, and to be safe he put it out for a corner. You can't blame him for that – better safe than sorry and all that – but it really cost us in the end. Sunderland took an outswinging corner and under Don Howe the tactic was to push out to catch their players offside. I was on the post and, as the ball came over, I came off it but Gordon Armstrong of Sunderland won a clean header and the ball went in the corner of the net. Beaten again and we were sick. If I had stayed on the post, I could have kept it out and you do start blaming yourself in that kind of situation.

The dressing room was dead quiet afterwards. Porterfield broke the silence when he asked me, 'Dennis, why did you step up?' Why? All I could say was that we always did that. It was all so depressing. What made it even more depressing was that Sunderland drew the team we wanted in the semi-finals, Norwich. We really thought we could beat them.

And so the season just drifted, like so many others. No league, no cups, more under-achievement. In truth you would have to say we weren't committed enough. We had some good – very good – players but it just didn't happen. And Ian Porterfield just wasn't strong enough to make it happen. A lot of the time he wanted to join in with the lads, be one of them and you can't do that as a manager. You have to keep your distance. There was a lack of discipline at Chelsea and that was summed up on an end-of-season trip to Canada in 1992. We had arranged to play in a tournament. The plane had landed and we were waiting for the bags to arrive. In one group there was me, Kerry Dixon, Andy Townsend, Vinnie Jones, Joe Allon – 'The Face' we used to call him – and Tony Cascarino. As we waited we saw one of those stretch limousines outside and after getting the luggage we decided to take it to the hotel and not bother with the team coach. We told Porterfield what we were going to do and he just said, 'Alright, see you there.' It was a disgrace really. Don Howe certainly wouldn't have allowed it. I remember that there were the lads from Dundee there too, playing in the same tournament. They were astonished at what we were allowed to get away with and must have thought we were a right load of flash gits. And they were right to, as well. A professional football team shouldn't be allowed to act like that.

But we had strong characters and basically we did what we wanted. We were sitting playing cards in the limo while the rest of the squad were waiting for bags and getting on the coach. We just treated it as an end-of-season jaunt, nothing too serious. Porterfield didn't say anything. It was as if he didn't want to upset anyone. He tried to be too close and would like to enjoy himself as well. If we were in some bar, he would join us for a few beers and that wasn't right. He should have distanced himself from us.

The following season came and it was much the same story. Porterfield showed early on that he just wanted to be close – too close – to us on a trip to Ireland. We were staying in Dublin and he came out with us one night. It was really getting on, very late, but he kept telling me to get behind the bar of this club and to keep pouring the beer. It was 3 a.m. and we were still going strong. Then we decided to get Kevin Wilson, one of the strikers at the club. Great lad Kevin, but we called him the tightest man in the world because he would never come out for a drink or buy one. He always refused point blank, so this night we decided to make him pay . . . by shaving off his treasured moustache.

It was really late when we got back to the hotel but we managed to find the master key. Then we all went back to our rooms to get ready for the invasion of Willo's room. The plan was for us to cover our heads in pillow cases with slots cut out for our eyes. We all assembled outside Willo's room and I had brought a razor to shave off his moustache. A bit dangerous that – I was still drunk as a skunk and it probably wasn't all that safe for me to have a razor in my hand. There were ten or twelve of us and, using the master key, we all dashed in and turned on the lights. He just sat up in bed stunned, his eyes staring like a rabbit's in car headlights. Alan Dickens, another quiet lad who had come out with us that night, looked on, totally baffled. Everyone held Willo down while I sat on him. 'Right, Willo, that moustache is coming off,' I said. He just looked up and there were tears in his eyes as he begged me not to do it. I don't think he was worried so much for his moustache as the rest of his face. In the state I was in, I would have cut him to ribbons. From nowhere, a bucket of freezing water suddenly drenched both of us and we all ran out and left him. I think it was also on that trip that I played a rotten trick on Tony Cascarino. His front teeth were false and he was always taking them out and leaving them around the place. One day I nicked them and he went mad looking for them. I coloured them black before returning them to him, and he went spare. But that was life at Chelsea at the time – a lot of laughing.

When the 1992-93 season started, it was in many ways a real non-event . . . again. Porterfield was beginning to feel the pressure and his man-management left a bit to be desired – as was seen in the Vinnie Jones transfer. Jonah was happy at Chelsea. He loved the fans and the feeling was mutual. But before we played up at Liverpool, Porterfield called him into his room at the hotel and told him he was being sold to Sheffield United. Harry Bassett wanted him and Chelsea had agreed to let him go. It was right out of the blue and I remember seeing Jonah that night and he looked really down. He told me what had happened. He was clearly in no frame of mind to play the next day – but he was picked, we lost and he was nothing like his usual self.

Another example of Porterfield's poor man-management was his treatment of Dave Beasant. Bes is a quality goalkeeper, there is no doubt in my mind about that. But a few Chelsea fans were getting on his back at the time, and it all came to a head in a league game against Norwich at Stamford Bridge in September 1992. We needed to win badly and we were comfortable enough at 2-0 up. Then came a disaster for Bes. He let in two soft goals and somehow we lost 2-3. After the match Porterfield told the press that it was the last game Bes would be playing for Chelsea. You shouldn't go public on things like that. It was like he was trying to keep on the side of the fans and staying in their good books, but you can't do that with players. You lose their respect. It was a silly thing to say as well because injuries might have meant he HAD to play Bes at some stage later in the season. What he said really hurt Bes. He is a very proud man and comments like those would have got to him. I am sure Porterfield said it without really thinking about the repercussions. All the punters turned on Bes and the manager lost a lot of the respect of the players over that incident. For me it was poor management. He put added pressure on Bes when what he wanted was for the pressure to be taken off him. Really, the writing was on the wall for Porterfield as the season went on. He didn't like the pressure on him – well, no one does really. But it's part and parcel of being at a big club, particularly one like Chelsea that has gone so long without success.

That season we felt we had a chance of winning the League Cup, or the Coca-Cola Cup as it was known in those days. We were drawn to play Crystal Palace at Selhurst Park in the fifth round and we had worked on a game plan with me playing in the hole just behind the strikers. But it didn't work out as we wanted – largely because we were playing on a swamp of a pitch. It was dreadful and the match should never have been played. To make matters worse, I had hurt the bridge of my foot in training the day before and I was really feeling it. I was knackered and had to pull out. We lost 3-1 and that was a real chance gone.

After that my foot began to give me a lot of grief. The physio, Bob Ward, couldn't find anything wrong and x-rays never showed anything up either. So I went to see Jenny Archer, the physio down at Wimbledon. I was willing to try anything and see anyone to get better and she told me to see this woman who looks after the fitness of the England hockey team. She found a bone out of alignment and manipulated it back into place by pulling my toes. She said that I would need to rest for a fortnight and I would be fine. But Ian Porterfield was desperate for results and, after I showed him I could run without any problem and kick a ball, he said I was playing against Aston Villa. That was the morning of the game and to be fair all went well. For me that is. There was no problem with the foot but we were losing 1-0. Then in the last minute I chased a ball, the Villa goalkeeper caught me and I was out for another four weeks.

That was it for Porterfield. He got the sack a few days later, in

February 1993, and I can't help thinking that the need to be stronger with the players played a part in his downfall. It didn't help that his number two, Stan Ternent, wasn't strong enough either. Like the manager, Stan was a decent bloke but he should have been harder. I had an argument with him at training once and, to put it crudely but accurately, he told me to 'piss off back to the dressing rooms'. I told him I wasn't going anywhere – or words to that effect – and suddenly it all went quiet as the rest of the players stood and watched what was happening in this blazing row. I had the right hump because he was talking to me like I was a little boy and I wasn't going to put up with that. Maybe I should have gone in but I didn't budge. Then Vinnie came over and told us both to pack it in. By then Stan was weakening. 'He has got to go in,' he kept saying and I kept refusing. So then he stormed off. 'Alright,' he said, 'I'll go in.' 'You go then,' I said. Porterfield saw everything that happened but just carried on. He didn't say anything. That shouldn't have happened. Ternent should have handled it differently. The lads were enjoying a five-a-side game at the time and, if he had stopped that and made them do running because of me, then I would have been under pressure to give way. They would have made me. If they had ordered me in, I would have gone, no question. But he was the one who buckled and that should never be the case. The player shouldn't win.

So it was no real surprise when Ian Porterfield went and, with him, Stan Ternent. The Chelsea players needed strong handling and Porterfield and Ternent didn't provide it.

We all wondered if the new man – Dave Webb – would be able to provide the leadership that we needed. He was accepted by the fans as manager because he had been part of that great team of the 1970s. He made it clear that he wanted to play the game in a certain way – with the ball pumped forward as early as possible. But I don't think the Chelsea supporters really liked that and the players weren't convinced either. Chelsea like to play with a bit of style. As it turned out, because of a combination of injuries and suspension, I didn't play that much for David Webb early on. But I will say he made us solid. We lost the first game, 2-1 at Blackburn, but we played, I would say, alright. Then we beat Arsenal 1-0 and stopped the rot. And Dave Beasant was back in goal.

I did find it strange that he sold Graeme Le Saux to Blackburn for £450,000. That was a very low price for a player that we later had to pay £5 million to get back to Chelsea. You would have to say that the cash we got for him was a little bit short. In exchange we got Steve Livingstone. With all due respect to Steve, no one knew anything about him. He was honest and hard working but not really special. Berge (our nickname for Graeme Le Saux who's from the Channel Islands and is called Bergerac after the television detective series) was a quality left-back or midfield player. At that time, he was a bit hot-headed and there was one famous – or infamous – incident when he threw his shirt at the bench after he was substituted during a game. That really got to the fans, they don't like to see anyone throwing the club shirt, it shows disrespect, and it made him unpopular for a time.

Graeme was a different bloke in those days. Now, since coming back, he has mellowed a lot and is one of the lads. But back then he had his mates – Kenny Monkou and Erland Johnsen – and they didn't really mix with the rest of us. They certainly stood up for each other, though. Vinnie Jones and Kenny Monkou almost came to blows once because Vinnie had a go at Berge, his big mate. Then Berge got in a ruck with Kerry Dixon and Erland got involved. Ian Porterfield stepped in to stop that one. The three of them stuck together and wouldn't go out boozing with the rest of us or anything like that. They were a bit different. There is nothing wrong with that. They just had a different mentality. When I look back, it probably did Berge a favour to leave at that time. He was frustrated at not getting a decent run of games in the team. When things went badly he always felt he was taking the blame and being dropped. He is a much more mature person now and a tremendous player. He always had ability and I remember Tony Cascarino saying to me the day Berge left, 'One day he will play left-back for England' – and he was spot on.

David Webb left at the end of the season. He was on trial as manager and, for whatever reason, the club decided against giving him the job full-time. As usual, we won nothing that season, and finished 11th in the table. I didn't get to know Webb all that well but I did have one run-in with him. As a joke, I had let off a fire extinguisher in the hotel we were staying in before an away match. He got the whole squad together and asked who had done it. No matter what anyone says about him, he did have a presence about him – he was the kind of man you didn't mess with. He said he would see us the following morning with the clear threat that, if the guilty party didn't own up, he would take appropriate action against all of us, a kind of collective blame thing. I went to see him later that evening and told him it was me. I think he suspected that anyway and he just looked straight at me and said, 'No more like that. You can have a laugh and joke but nothing as stupid as that again. Alright?' And I got the message.

You certainly knew where you stood with Webb. I was never sure of him as a manager and I don't think he fancied me as a player really. Whether I would have stayed if he had stayed we will never know because at the start of the next season, 1993-94, we had a new manager in Glenn Hoddle. It was the start of a new era for Chelsea, there is no doubt about that.

Chapter 11

glenn hoddle

I had played against Glenn Hoddle a few times and was as aware as anyone that he was a quality player, technically very talented. I met him two years before he joined us when he came to Chelsea for treatment while he was playing for Monaco. We'd say hello to each other in the morning and he seemed a nice enough bloke but we certainly didn't get to know each other well. He had a much bigger impact on my life when he joined Chelsea as player-manager in 1993 to succeed David Webb.

Hoddle came to Chelsea from Swindon where he had done a fantastic job, taking them to the Premiership through the play-offs. Expectations of him were high at Chelsea but his first signings were, well, mixed. There were clearly financial restrictions on him and he bought players who he knew from the First Division – like Mark Stein and Paul Furlong. He also signed Gavin Peacock from Newcastle. Steiny did well for us and Gavin was magnificent, a really good player. But poor Paul had a bad time. At a certain level he was a good and effective player but in the Premiership I feel he was found wanting.

Hoddle also sold Andy Townsend, the club captain at the time, and I was gutted about that. Andy was – and still is – an excellent player . . . strong, a decent passer and someone who can run all day. I was a bit disillusioned when Andy was sold but Hoddle then called me in and made me captain. Well, temporary captain anyway. He said, 'I'm putting you on trial to see how you go.' It seemed he wasn't totally convinced that I was the right choice but felt I was worth a go. It wasn't exactly a vote of confidence.

When he told me I was on trial, it seemed like he thought he was doing me a great favour. That is not the way you should go about making someone captain. The responsibility should be given to someone you believe in, not someone you feel should be on trial. It almost seemed that at the back of his mind, he didn't really want me to be captain. You appoint a captain because you think he is the right man but I never felt he had confidence in me.

I never got to know Hoddle as a person, even when I was his captain and saw him almost every day of my life. He was a strange guy, more than a bit distant and you couldn't get to the bottom of him, find out what made him tick. He always kept his cards close to his chest and wouldn't really say much to the players. In his first season, we didn't do all that well in the league and all he kept saying was, 'You're playing well, just keep it up, you have been unlucky.' It seemed to me he wanted the players to be on his side and to like him but I had already seen with other managers at Chelsea that this isn't the best way to work. You have to upset people if you are going to be successful.

If we lost he would moan a bit, and he would be the same in training. When players couldn't do what he wanted them to do he would get the right hump. You could hear him tutting and sighing – as if everyone should be blessed with his talent. He seemed to lose sight of the fact that not all players were as gifted as he was. Not all players are like Glenn Hoddle – they have the ability to do different things and play in a different way. That doesn't mean they can't contribute to the team and Hoddle seemed to forget that he had needed people alongside him at Tottenham – people like Graham Roberts – to do the things that he couldn't. When one of our players failed to do what he wanted in the way he wanted, there would be this sigh, this real put-down. You just knew what he was thinking.

Then we had our first real bust-up. The season had started badly for us and we were playing Southampton down at The Dell just after

Christmas. We were third from bottom and there was a real fear that we would go down. I was seriously cheesed off about it – and it didn't help when we lost 3-1 that day. I was steaming, really depressed, and all I could hear Hoddle saying in the dressing room afterwards was how unlucky we had been. 'Just keep going, you will be alright. Does anyone want to say anything?' 'Yes, I do,' I said. 'I want to say something.' He asked me what I wanted to say and all my frustrations of the previous few months came out. 'If we go on as we are,' I said, 'we are going to be the unluckiest team to be relegated. What we have to do is start putting our foot in and try to win games.' He looked a bit stunned that someone should say that. 'Oh,' he said, 'you think that's the way to win football matches, do you?' 'No, but it is the way to get out of relegation trouble.' 'So you think that's the way to play, by kicking people?' We were never going to agree. We were such different people. Me, I would do anything to win a game. Hoddle was more of a purist.

Peter Shreeves, Hoddle's assistant, tried to step in as some kind of referee to calm things down and end the argument. 'I think what he is trying to say, Glenn, is that we have to try that bit harder and get stuck in a bit more,' he said. But it didn't really help and I took my shorts off, then the rest of my kit and went into the shower. We were getting nowhere. I was so uptight and upset that I remember telling Hoddle to f . . . off as I walked into the shower. He said, 'Go on, have a shower, walk away.' I swore at him again. It was a real row and it was as well for me that I was playing reasonably well at the time. If I hadn't been, then the exchange of views might well have cost me my place in the team.

That was the first of many arguments with Hoddle. There just wasn't the kind of mutual respect that you expect between a manager and captain. In fact, I always had the feeling that I was made captain only because I had a great rapport with the players, the fans and the chairman Ken Bates. There was never any kind of conference between us, I was never able to knock on his door and discuss things with him, ask him what he felt about this or that. He just wouldn't let me.

Some people said he was arrogant. Well, he would certainly do his own thing, do things his own way and basically that was that. I think that the most I ever said to him on a daily basis was 'Good morning'. To put it another way, Hoddle was more than a bit stand-offish, a bit aloof. He knew what he wanted to do and felt no need or reason to explain it to other people.

What I will say, though, on the positive side, was that he changed the whole profile of Chelsea Football Club. The dressing rooms at the training ground were cold, damp places, but he really spruced them up. At one time, you just didn't want to go in them but he made them a lot more comfortable. And he changed a lot of other things too. When we used to travel for away games, everyone would turn up how they wanted, dressed in what they felt was comfortable. We also stayed in hotels that weren't exactly five-star – not dumps but definitely not the best. Hoddle changed all that. We were given club suits and stayed at much better hotels. That was a welcome change and he laid the foundations for us to become the club we are now. We went on to better things and that was not a coincidence. In his career at Tottenham and Monaco, he had the best and now he wanted that for us. He felt Chelsea was a major club and should also have the best. He made the club put its hand in its pocket more and, in that sense, he made the club a success and he must be given credit for that. Under Hoddle, we became more professional; there is no question of that. His determination to get what he wanted paid off – he wanted better and got it.

On the field in that first season the story in the league was the same as I had always known it – we just drifted along, most of the time in the wrong half of the table and never threatening the teams at the top. But the FA Cup turned out to be a different story.

If you are going to be successful in the FA Cup, it really does help if you have good draws and we certainly couldn't complain that season. In the third round, we were drawn against Barnet who, co-incidentally, Hoddle's brother Carl played for. We made hard work of the game and they took us to a replay. Both games were played at Stamford Bridge but eventually we went through comfortably enough. We were then on the road to the club's first major final in almost 25 years.

No one seemed too concerned about the league by that stage. We were pulling away from the relegation area and it was the cup that we had our sights on. In that run we also played Oxford and Wolves. The only really difficult draw was against Sheffield Wednesday in the fourth round, and after that it went very kindly for us. In the semi-final we played Luton at Wembley. They were a division below us and I always felt we would beat them. We won 2-0 but in truth we were worth more than that. Kerry Dixon, my old friend from Chelsea, was at Luton at the time and I felt for him. You feel for your pals in football but you have to be self-centred and, to be brutal, I wanted to get to that final more than him. On the day, we were much better than they were. We all played at our best, Chelsea were in the FA Cup final and everyone was saying how well Glenn Hoddle had done in his first season. And you have to give him credit; he did get us there and did well for us. He certainly won over the fans with that achievement and they were very much on his side. The league performances may have been indifferent to say the least but we had given the fans a day out at Wembley in one of the most prestigious competitions for the first time in a long, long time and they were delirious.

The final itself was a wash-out, literally. It didn't just rain on our parade, it hammered down. We played Manchester United and we were thumped 4-0, slaughtered on a miserable afternoon on which the rain never stopped. For an hour or so we matched them. It might have been a different story had a shot by Gavin Peacock gone in instead of hitting the bar and coming out. He hit a superb volley, really sweetly but, when that didn't go in, I think we knew deep down that it wasn't going to be our day.

Maybe we had used up all our luck in the draws that got us to the final. Anyway, soon after half-time, United got a penalty. I did my best to make sure Eric Cantona didn't score – I had a bet with him. I had used the tactic before when Tony Cottee was about to take a penalty for Everton. As he stood waiting to take it I said, 'I bet you a fiver you miss.' He just said, 'Piss off, leave me alone.' But I kept on and on to him: 'Come on, let's have a bet.' Whether it affected him or not I don't know, but I do know that he missed. Psychological warfare and verbals go on all the time in football. You just want to give yourself an edge. Having succeeded once, I thought I would try it again with Cantona. 'Come on,' I said, 'let's have a bet. I bet you miss.' I was a bit taken aback when he said, 'Okay, £100.' I was thinking more in terms of another fiver but I still agreed. He scored. Later in the game United got another penalty. This time he came up to me and said, 'Hey, double or quits on the £100?' 'No chance,' I said. And, of course, he put that one away too.

After the game, I gave the £100 to Paul Parker, United's right-back, to give to Cantona. Next season, Paul came to play with us at Chelsea and I asked him if he had given Cantona the cash. He said, 'Yes and Eric said thank you. He said you are a good man and to thank you very much.'

I really rated Cantona. He was class, a very talented guy. He was a really great player who ruled the roost at Manchester United. He did what he wanted to do and he did it really well. His control of a football was phenomenal. I remember him playing at Stamford Bridge once and at one point during the game we were just glad to clear the ball. It went as far as the touchline and we thought we were safe. But you were never safe with Cantona around. He suddenly produced a volley that no one was expecting and the ball bounced over Dmitri Kharine in our goal. Fortunately, the ball hit the bar and Dmitri caught the rebound. It would have been one of the most spectacular goals ever. I just watched and said, 'Bloody Hell.' But that is what Cantona could do. He was instinctive and extremely gifted. He could make the ball do what he wanted.

Anyway, in that final, United won at a canter. I remember Hoddle saying before the game that he had a dream that, as player-manager, he would come on when we were losing and score. That's why he made himself substitute for the final. Well, he was half right. He came on alright but he didn't score. Hoddle used to think he could do the job as sweeper, and that no one else could play in that position, and he did turn out for us in that role a few times that season. But, to put it diplomatically, I don't think he was the world's most natural defender. He played sweeper against Liverpool at Anfield in a league game and Ian Rush murdered him.

That FA Cup final was beyond his recall or anyone else's. We were overwhelmed and to this day I haven't watched the video of that game. I can't face it. It should be one of my most prized possessions, you know, the day I led Chelsea out at Wembley for the FA Cup final. But I can't bring myself to do it. The gulf between the two sides was never more apparent than on that day. Nowadays you can look back and see how far Chelsea have come but I refuse to watch that video. In fact, by now, I may even have thrown it away. That's how bad I felt. The game proved to me that you can only go so far without real, genuine class – and we didn't have as much as Manchester United. Thanks to the draws we had through the competition we reached Wembley without too many problems but we just couldn't compete with Manchester United once they got ahead of us.

It was a black day.

Chapter 12

hard times

I finished the season as captain, despite the row I had with Hoddle at Southampton earlier on. Clearly he didn't hold it against me but I also reckon he needed me. I was a regular member of the team, I had played well that season and I was a strong character. He needed me alright and he can have had no complaints about my form while he was my manager at Chelsea.

The next season, 1994-95, however, was a personal disaster – without doubt the worst of my time at Chelsea. We had qualified for European football because Manchester United had won the league as well as the FA Cup and were in the Champions League which put us, as cup runners-up, in the Cup Winners' Cup. We reached the semi-final and went out to Real Zaragoza but we were never at full strength at any time. At that time, UEFA had a rule restricting the amount of foreign players – and the Welsh, Irish and Scottish players were all regarded as foreign. It meant that Hoddle had to be very selective about who he picked and, to be fair, he did well to get us to the last four.

On top of that, I played very few games. I had a lot of injury problems, particularly with my thigh, and there was also THAT court case to contend with. It was a dreadful time for me, especially when Hoddle took the captaincy from me.

Perhaps my court case was the excuse he was looking for to take the armband away; maybe he felt he had to be seen to be doing the right thing. But I look at it differently. Sometimes in football you have to stick by players, to show solidarity with them, and not do what everyone thinks is the right thing. Everyone seems to be demanding one course of action but I feel there are occasions when you say, 'No, I don't care. I am sticking by my player. What's done is done. When the real truth of what happened comes out, then I will do something about it.' I felt Hoddle should have stood by me until he knew the full facts.

Hoddle didn't get too involved in the court case at first because no one at Chelsea thought for one minute that I was going to go to prison. That soon changed when I was sentenced. The last thing the club needed was to be without me. The team weren't doing fantastically well in the league and we were still involved in European football. To put it bluntly, they needed me to play.

At that time, playing football was a fantastic escape for me. Out there on the pitch was the one place when I could put everything behind me. Off the field, I had all these pressures to contend with, what with the danger of going to prison and everyone wanting to talk about it. When I was playing, nothing could touch me or reach me. It was brilliant. But in December came a real blow when I badly injured my thigh against Liverpool. I was in a bad way and the assessment of the medical people was that I would be out for a minimum of six weeks.

That did my brain in. Suddenly, the place where I could escape, the one place where I could feel at ease – the football pitch – was out of bounds. All I could do was sit on the treatment table and worry. The court case was coming closer, and with no football to look forward to, all I could do was brood. To make matters worse, when I tried to play, I tore the muscle again. The season was going from very bad to much worse. I later discovered that I should have had an operation right away but instead I continued having treatment – including my first meeting with the faith healer Eileen Drewery.

She took a lot of flack from people after Hoddle's resignation from the England job but I found Eileen Drewery to be a lovely lady who really meant well. It was Hoddle's idea that I meet her. 'You should see her, she may well be able to help,' he said to me. 'But you have to go there with an open mind.' I couldn't see what I had to lose. I had tried everything else.

To be honest, I have never been a great believer in that kind of thing, that someone could lay their hands on your leg and heal you. Maybe that's why it didn't work. Perhaps it only succeeds if you are totally convinced it will. I met Eileen and the first thing I remember is how welcome she made me feel. I went to her house, we had a chat and she made me a cup of tea. She told me to relax and, to be fair, I felt completely at ease. She put her hands on my head, then on my neck and told me to lie down on the sofa. She told me she was going to give me some healing and put her hand on my injured leg. Then she went into a kind of trance. She told me to close my eyes. To be perfectly honest, I didn't know what to say. I had never experienced anything like it. It lasted for a couple of minutes and she then said that she was going to give me what she called 'absent healing'. She said she would think of me and try to help me.

As far as I can see, Eileen Drewery is a genuinely caring woman who doesn't mean any harm to anyone. I don't know if she can heal people but I know she wants to. Her treatment didn't work for me but that's not to say it's the same for everyone. I felt for her during all the fuss about her involvement with the England players. From my experience she is one of the most genuine and honest people I have met. She cares about people and there is nothing wrong with that. If she can help, she will. The way she has been made to look like some crank just isn't right and it isn't fair. I thought she was really nice. In fact she reminded me of my mum.

The only answer to my injury problem was to have surgery – but that caused some panic at the club because the appeal against my sentence was coming up. After the operation to cure the thigh muscle injury I would need the right treatment and the right rehabilitation – and I wouldn't have got that if I had been sent to prison. The new physiotherapist at the club, Mike Banks, was very worried.

I had the operation and I was left with a huge scar on my thigh. I had a right go at the surgeon when I saw it. He told me the scar would only be a small one, a couple of inches at most. But it was about five times that size. I went mad until the surgeon explained what had happened. Apparently, there was a hole in my thigh and it had bled, leaving a lot of blood running down the muscle. This had dried and had to be cleared out. If the operation had been done right away, I would have been back comparatively quickly. Instead, I wasted three or four months trying to get it right. At least it was going to get better now – and everything else seemed to be getting better too.

Chapter 13

two legends

The verdict in the court case was quashed and at last there was some light at the end of the season when Hoddle decided to give me back the captaincy. That was another boost. I still felt it was wrong for him to take it off me in the first place but he obviously thought it was the right thing to do and I had to accept that. And in the summer of 1995 Hoddle changed the face of football at Chelsea for ever by bringing two legends to Stamford Bridge.

For different reasons, Ruud Gullit and Mark Hughes were two of the players that I respected most in the game and it was a tremendous coup for Hoddle to sign them for Chelsea. They represented a turning point for the club and for Glenn Hoddle. It was Hoddle's status that helped attract Ruud and Hughesie to Chelsea and the club certainly went up in everyone's estimation when they arrived. People had to take notice of Chelsea now. It was clear that we didn't want to be also-rans any more, that we meant business.

Ruud was one of the greatest players I have ever seen, a terrific athlete who had achieved so much in the world game. Hughesie was the player you never wanted to be against you. Defenders hate him. He was talented and bloody hard. At his peak he was one of the best strikers in Europe, no question. And he was still a quality player when he came to Chelsea from Manchester United.

Off the field Hughesie is really quiet. He will have a laugh and joke with the lads and will join in with everything but he's not loud or aggressive. On the pitch he will lose his head in an instant. It wouldn't bother him one bit to stamp on you or whack you. You know exactly where he is coming from and what to expect. That is precisely what people don't like. He is a strong person, mentally and physically. It is impossible to intimidate him. He is like a pocket battleship. He is what I would call a proper man – not afraid to stand up and fight his corner. You just can't scare him. I used to hate it when I played against him. You would want to boot him so much. But, even if you did, he would come back for more – and give you some back.

There was one game I played in between Wimbledon and Manchester United down at Plough Lane when Hughesie scored the winner. As he ran back, he threw the ball at Keith Curle, who had been trying to give him a bad time the whole game. Curley booted the ball back at him. Then Hughesie ran by me and I kicked him and tried to push him. He just swatted me away. You just couldn't hurt him no matter what you tried and it niggles opponents no end. I was just glad to have him on my side for a change.

The first of the pair I met was Ruud. I was in the treatment room having work on my thigh after the operation when this bloody great Yeti came in. I was one of the first players to welcome him to the club. 'Great to have you here,' I said. 'You're a legend.' The immediate impression he made on me was that he was laid back and relaxed; and that never changed in all his time at Chelsea. He also knew all about my problems, both on and off the pitch. He asked how my leg was coming on and was pleased to hear that all my trouble off the field had been sorted out. Then he went off for his medical.

But it was soon obvious to me that Ruud was too big a person for Hoddle to handle. Ruud had this aura and presence about him – he had everything, he had done everything and there is not too much you can say to a person like that – as Hoddle found out when we played Wimbledon in the FA Cup that season. All week we had prepared to combat the Wimbledon style of play. Footballs were thrown up into the air and we had to deal with them. The only words we heard all week were Wimbledon, Wimbledon and more bloody Wimbledon. All our work was centred on how they would play. I could see Ruud wasn't too happy about it because he felt we were giving them an advantage concentrating on them rather than rehearsing what we did best.

To be honest, we didn't play well at all in that match and we drew 2-2. Hoddle had us in the following morning, Sunday, for a team meeting. We all sat down to talk about the game. Hoddle said his piece and then Ruud said, 'I do not agree with this. All we have done is concentrate on Wimbledon and what they can do. We should concentrate on what WE can do. We are a far better team than Wimbledon and we have better players but all you want to do is concern yourself with them. All week you have the ball in the air. That was not the right approach.' Hoddle disagreed and turned to me for support, 'Dennis, what do you think?' He wasn't best pleased with my response. 'I agree with everything Ruud has said. I think he's right.'

Hoddle wasn't happy with me disagreeing with him, not in front of all the other lads. He was looking for back-up and didn't get it. But I only spoke the truth and reflected what the other players felt. I don't think Hoddle could forget things like that. He insisted he had done things the right way to prepare for the game. I still said we should concentrate on what we are going to do and that turned out to be the plan for the replay. We won – comfortably, I might say – 3-1. And we played really well.

That season we reached the FA Cup semi-final and met that lot from Manchester United again. This time, though, there was going to be no 4-0 repeat from two seasons earlier. The match was at Villa Park and Ruud put us ahead with a great header after Hughesie had set up the chance. Half-time and we were still ahead. We weren't dominating them or anything like that but we were doing okay. We didn't look in too much trouble but we knew, with the talent they had in the team, that we had to get that vital second goal. We failed and paid the price. One sloppy back-pass from Craig Burley and United were level through David Beckham and, once they were back on terms, they went for it. Beckham scored again and then we had to chase the game. There was a chance for us late on but an effort from John Spencer was cleared off the line by, of all people, Eric Cantona – just about the last person you would expect to find on his own goal-line.

That was our last chance of any success that season gone and, as you would expect, it was a very quiet dressing room afterwards. Poor Craig was inconsolable, blaming himself for the United equaliser. He'd done a similar thing against Coventry a few weeks earlier and it's strange how, once a player makes a bad mistake like that, he keeps repeating it. But no one blamed him. Craig was a very good player, very under-rated, and one who had done a lot to get us to the semi-final. He was devastated. But no fingers were pointed. These things happen in football and it's no good blaming each other afterwards. If you lose, you lose together. That is how it should be. You only blame people if they haven't tried and there is no way in the world you could accuse Craig of being a non-trier. He made a genuine mistake, nothing more and nothing less.

That was to be Hoddle's last chance of success with Chelsea. In the league we were mid-table once again and before the end of the season we all knew that he was going to be the next England manager. Terry Venables had been told that he was not going to have his contract extended after the Euro 96 finals and Hoddle was appointed as his successor after the championships. He was at the end of his contract at Stamford Bridge and the club gave him the go-ahead to talk to the Football Association. A lot of people at the club were disappointed with him for going but he didn't walk out on an agreement. Before he left, he called the players in one by one to say his goodbyes. To me he just said, 'Thanks for the way you have played for me and for what you have done for me. Just carry on with what you are doing. And all the best in the future.' From that moment, from what he said and the way he said it, I knew that I wouldn't be playing for him in his new job. And really that's the last time I spoke to him.

I once said – in answer to a question at a press conference about playing for England – that I didn't think Hoddle would ever pick me for an international while he was in charge. I wasn't speaking off the top of my head. As well as falling out with me at Chelsea, and not liking me disagreeing with him, I don't think Hoddle particularly rated me as a player. I sensed that he felt Chelsea was about as far as I would ever go as a player. He didn't like my style of playing or fancy me as a player. But I don't have a problem with that – that's his opinion and that is fair enough. While he was at Chelsea I know I did alright for him but I knew deep down inside that, when he got the job as England manager, he would never include me in his plans.

Not everyone agreed. Terry Byrne is the masseur at Chelsea and Hoddle drafted him on to the England back-up team when he took over the national side. Terry loves Glenn to bits and he said to me, 'You'll be the first he'll pick.' I just said, 'I won't be in there, no way. I have done okay for him but he doesn't like the way I play and, to be honest, he doesn't think I'm good enough.' He told me not to be stupid and had a £10 bet with me that I would be called up into Hoddle's first England squad. Yes, he paid up. He was clearly under the impression that Hoddle and I got on and possibly other people thought the same. But we didn't talk as manager and captain and clearly he didn't have enough respect for me as a person or player.

To sum Hoddle up, I would say he tried to be cagey all the time. He didn't want anyone to know what he regarded as secrets. Maybe he was trying to fool the opposition and give his own team every advantage. If that was the objective, then I can understand his point. But he wouldn't tell anyone the full script. He certainly wouldn't give away too many clues about what he was thinking. He would also put out false information about injuries and he's not the only manager to do that. Some players – because we are a superstitious lot – aren't too comfortable with that but that is the way he would do things, though I have to say that he never did that with me. He liked his own way and felt what he said should go.

There was a situation when we reached the FA Cup final in 1994 and, as is the case with every club, we wanted to set up a players' pool in order to share out the money we earned through publicity and promotions. I put forward my agent, Eric Hall, to do it and the rest of the players went along with that. But Hoddle never liked Eric and said he wanted someone else. We spoke about it and I insisted that Eric was the man we wanted, chosen by the players' committee. Hoddle just didn't want him around the players but eventually he reluctantly suffered it. At every opportunity, though, he would have a go at Eric about things he set up for the players but they stuck by me and Hoddle had to let it go.

Hoddle is certainly a strong character; there is no denying that. When he resigned as England manager my first reaction was, 'He would not have wanted to resign.' I know that much about him. That job meant so much to him. I am certain it would have really hurt him to resign. When his contract was up at Chelsea he left for what he regarded as THE job. He is the type of person who likes to be the centre of attention, totally in charge. The England job provided that kind of stage and was the one he was waiting for and looking for. In my opinion, the job was perfect for him. Hoddle was single-minded enough to handle all that goes with the international scene. Despite our differences, I thought at the time he was the right person and he didn't do badly. But it was always going to be hard to follow a class act like Terry Venables.

Chapter 14

england, terry venables and gazza

As I have said already it was a marvellous feeling for me when I made my international debut for England out in Turkey in 1990. For a start, I was delighted to be chosen for the squad. I didn't think I would even make that, to be honest. I was just a couple of months into my career at Chelsea and, although I had started quite well at my new club, my form hadn't been the greatest approaching the European Championship qualifier. A lot of eyebrows were raised when Graham Taylor picked me for the squad and he showed a lot of common sense when he allocated me a room with John Barnes.

Barnesy was an established England player while I was the new-comer and Graham Taylor knew it would help me settle in quicker. I have to say Barnesy was quality. He spoke to me like I had been his team-mate all his life, made me feel welcome and generally made me relax. It could have been difficult for me and there was every reason for me to feel jittery but Barnesy helped me through that difficult period.

When we reached the stadium on the day of the game the first thing I really sensed was how hostile the environment was. Actually, my sister Kim had come over to see the game. She had a friend who worked for British Airways and had managed to get cheap fares over to Turkey at the last minute. I didn't even know she was there – luckily. If I had known I would have been worried sick about her.

In the dressing room I was quiet, very different from how I usually was before a match at Wimbledon or Chelsea. They were new sur-roundings for me and I just wanted to stay focused and concentrated on what I had to do when I went out on the park. I just listened and took in what Graham Taylor and his assistant Lawrie McMenemy were telling me.

As we went out it was Stuart Pearce who gave it the big battle cry. He'd hardly said a word as we were getting ready but I think everyone in the stadium must have heard him as we went out of the dressing room.

It really does make the hairs on the back of your neck bristle when they play 'God Save the Queen' before the match and you are singing along. Of course, it's better at Wembley because the vast majority of the crowd are behind you but it is still special when you are abroad. I can remember their fans being very hostile and making a lot of noise and urging the Turks on with a lot of passion. They were a hard side – not into any underhand tricks or spitting, nothing like that – just a good, strong team and I learned a lot that day.

One thing I learned was the speed needed to succeed at international level. Everything around you seems to happen that much faster and you have to be quick on your feet and in your head. It made it all the more satisfying that I scored the winning goal in what was a vital win in our qualifying group. For me it was a great experience and a very proud day, one I will never forget. The whole episode – selection, travelling, playing from the start, scoring – was a significant part of my education in football. I was delighted for myself and for my whole family.

Right up until a month or so before the European Championships were held in England in 1996, I thought I was in with a good chance of making the final squad. In the end it wasn't to be. I didn't make the cut. Upset? Yes, of course. It was the biggest football tournament to be held in England for 30 years and it would have been marvellous to be part of it. But bitter? No, not at all. The reason was Terry Venables. I had so much time and respect for that man it was untrue. I respected him more than Glenn Hoddle and indeed more than any other man I have worked with in football. He is class, quality and extremely loyal. He is a good man and a wonderful coach.

I was sorry to see Venables deprived of the chance to carry on after Euro 96 because I think he would have done a tremendous job with the England team. He was, by far in my opinion, the best man for the job. And if anyone has grounds for a grudge against him, it's me. I was one of the four people who were told in Hong Kong just before the tournament that I wasn't going to be in the final squad. But I didn't feel one bit of resentment towards him, not one. Why? Because Terry Venables is a man who sticks by his players, who shows faith in them when things get a bit rough . . . as he did with me when I had my off-the-field troubles with the taxi driver. I had been in every squad up until then but after the court case, when I had been sentenced, he pulled me out of the squad. He explained that it was not good for him, for the Football Association, for the squad or for me to stay part of it in those circumstances. But he also promised me that when everything had been sorted out, I would be in his next squad.

As well as the court case I had problems with the serious thigh injury in 1994 and it wasn't until the next season, 1995-96, that I got playing again. And come the first England squad selection after that, sure enough I was in it. Terry Venables wouldn't have picked me out of sentiment. I hadn't been one of his players at club level and often, when a manager changes jobs and moves to take over the national team, he will rely heavily on the players that he knows. He is familiar with them, is aware of their strengths and weaknesses and, if you like, knows what he is getting. There is a trust, a bond between them. I wasn't one of those players although he must have rated me as a player because he tried to sign me for Tottenham seven years earlier after Wimbledon won the FA Cup. And it seems he still did because I was a regular part of his squads when he took over with England.

I know it upset Venables when he left me out of the final squad for Euro 96. He made his decision in Hong Kong, where we had ended up after a short tour in which we had played two matches. He looked very sombre when he called me into his room and said, 'Dennis, I am sorry, but I am not taking you. You won't be in the final squad.' I don't think he anticipated my reaction. Maybe he thought I be would angry but all

I said was, 'Boss, I just want to thank you for including me in so many squads. Honestly, I really enjoyed it and thanks again. It's okay, not a problem.' Terry looked really taken aback by what I said. I don't think he could believe it and all he said was, 'Dennis, just piss off. Go. I am really gutted at having to give you that news.'

When I left the room the other lads were there to console me. He had left out four of us: Phil Neville, Peter Beardsley, Robert Lee and myself. The rest of the players came up to us, put their arms round us and tried to make us feel better. But, truthfully, I didn't need that much consoling. I remember Don Howe, Terry's assistant, coming up to me and saying, 'Look, that was really nice what you said. I've spoken to Terry and he was really upset at having to leave you out and the way you accepted it was brilliant.' I just repeated that I was grateful to Terry for picking me in the first place.

I am as patriotic as the next man and wearing that England shirt meant a lot to me. I will never forget what I reckon was my best game for England in a friendly against Nigeria in 1994. I took the free-kick from which David Platt scored and it was a triumph for me and for Terry. We proved a few people wrong that night. There were those who didn't think I should be in the England set-up because I wasn't good enough and others who thought I should have missed out because of the problems I experienced off the pitch. But Terry, as I said, was loyal. He was under pressure to leave me out but he didn't, and that meant a lot to me.

It didn't go unnoticed by the other players either. They loved Terry for the way he stuck by them and players respond to that kind of manager. He never criticises players in public, or indeed when they are together as a group. He will do it privately, man-to-man, face-to-face. That earns respect. He is what I would call 'a players' man'. Everyone was treated the same, we were all on the same level and I have to say that, while I will always be grateful to Graham Taylor for giving me my chance with England, I enjoyed working with Terry Venables more. He has this knack of making everyone feel at ease and welcome. When you first join up with England, you can't help but feel a bit self-conscious and nervous. That is only natural. But under Terry any new players always felt very soon that they had always been in there, that they had been involved for years. He really did generate a great spirit among the lads.

The two players that I became close to in my time playing for England were Teddy Sheringham and Paul Gascoigne. Gazza likes to enjoy himself and is seriously funny. We needed him not just for his ability but also because of his character. He is a fantastic person to have about because there is no doubt that he livens the place up. He just doesn't care and he makes everyone relax and feel at ease with his personality. Yes, he does silly things and pulls stupid pranks. With Gazza around, you can expect to get pepper in your dessert and it has been known for him to book a sun-bed for one of the black players in the squad.

I really felt for Gazza when he was left out of the World Cup squad in 1998. I know what England meant to him and I knew that he would be devastated. What actually happened, what the real reason was for him being left out, I don't know. But I do know that he is the kind of player with the talent and class to open doors, to break a deadlock and, for me, you take players like that to the World Cup Finals.

It was Gazza who was heavily involved in a row over damage caused on the plane bringing the squad back from Hong Kong on that pre-Euro 96 tour to the Far East. The way it sounded when we got back was as if the whole interior of the plane had been ripped apart. At the time, the lads all went for the 'collective responsibility' approach. If one player had been singled out, then all hell could have been let loose. There would have been enormous pressures on the Football Association and Terry Venables to leave the culprit out of the squad. That was the last thing Terry could have done with at such a crucial time in his preparations. And there has been endless speculation about what happened that day. Well, here's the truth.

Gazza is not the best of flyers and he gets very nervous and uptight on a plane. So he had a few drinks. I'm not saying he was drunk, he had just had a few drinks to calm his nerves, as, I am sure, many people do. When we were airborne Gazza tried to slide out the television attached to his seat. He pulled it the wrong way and it broke. Honestly, it was no major thing and I am sure he is not the only person that kind of thing has happened to.

When we landed, he went to get his holdall from the luggage locker above the seat. There were all sorts of stories going about at the time – including one that I was up there asleep. What nonsense. What happened was that Gazza's bag was stuck tight and he couldn't get it out. I went to help him and as we both pulled it the locker spring broke. Again, I am sure that has happened before but, because it was the England football squad, a huge fuss was made about it when we got home. There were no pressmen on the plane and all the publicity came about because the airline – Cathay Pacific – put out a statement about it. Surely they could have quietly gone to the Football Association and told them about the damage – which I can assure you was accidental – and asked them to pay for it without telling the world.

There was also a lot made of the 'dentist's chair' night out in Hong Kong before we came home but again, that was made to look a lot worse than it actually was. We had been given the night off and went to this club. It was Gazza's birthday and we had a good few drinks to celebrate. But we were in a corner of the bar and we all kept ourselves to ourselves, not bothering anyone else.

Okay, maybe we did have a bit too much to drink but nothing really got out of hand. Because it was Gazza's birthday, as a joke we ripped his shirt. That set him off and he started saying that because it was his birthday, everyone had to have a ripped shirt. So he went round doing exactly that. Teddy and myself also caught Gazza out on the phone. We thought we'd lost him but then we spotted him in a phone booth round the corner. Behind the bar were a pair of boxing gloves and Teddy and myself took one each, jumped on Gazza and started laying in to him. He didn't know what was happening. It was a laugh, no one got hurt, it was just a lads' night out.

I accept that we were over there representing England and the celebrations may have gone a little over-the-top. Yes, we had a go in the dentist's chair, where they pour vodka down your throat, and everyone was up for it. All we were doing, though, was letting our hair down and unwinding because the next day we were going to find out who would be in the squad for Euro 96. But we meant no harm and, although we had the night off, we were given a time to be back at our hotel and no one was late.

Yes, we were making a bit of noise but we weren't bothering anyone else or spoiling it for anyone else. One bloke did come over and asked Bryan Robson to tone it down but Robbo just said that we were enjoying ourselves, doing no harm and that, if the bloke thought it was too rowdy, he should go back over to the other side of the bar.

Generally it was people coming over to us and asking for autographs and photos, which we were only too happy to give. A few people, though, were a bit naughty. They saw the chance to make a few bob and cashed in by selling the photos to newspapers. They seemed genuine at the time and all we were doing was obliging. It was one of those situations where we couldn't win in many ways. If we had said no photographs, they would have complained. Because we said yes, and we gave them pictures, they cashed in and made us look terrible. Right out of order. It shows you what some people will do to cash in on footballers.

After being left out of the Euro 96 squad, I went away on holiday. I watched the finals on television and really wanted to be out there. It was very frustrating. I would have loved to have been part of it but at least I can say I was part of the build-up. And I stress, once again, there are no grudges on my part. Terry Venables made what he thought was the correct decision in the make-up of his squad and I wasn't part of it. It seems that Jamie Redknapp and Nick Barmby, who had scored two goals against China, got the nod over me and good luck to them. I have no problem with that or with Terry. He is the best man-manager I had worked for, bar none. He knows how to get the best out of people and I also had a lot of time for his assistant Don Howe. To me they made a great partnership for England and it was a privilege to work with them.

It was a great experience playing with England's top footballers, and it was a very lucrative experience to be in the squad with Gazza. He's one hell of a man – but useless at cards. I wasn't the only one to benefit, not by a long way. We all did. He just can't bluff at cards.

We played cards to pass the time and one of the games we played was brag. It is a three-card game and takes a lot of nerve. You can go blind, in other words not look at your cards, and, whatever you bet, someone who has seen their cards – or gone 'open' – has to double your stake. Gazza was always chasing his money and it was never long before he went blind, just to increase the pot. Eventually, he would look at his hand – and we knew exactly what he had. If it was a bad one, he would look to the person sitting next to him, if they were out, show his hand and ask, 'What do you reckon? Yes, I think so too. I will go on.' Of course the rest of us still in did as well because we knew he had a poor hand. After one go, he would stack his cards. If he had a good hand when he picked them up, he would have this twitch in his right shoulder and show his cards to no one. Immediately the rest of us threw our cards in and to this day, he can't work out how we knew he could beat the rest of us.

Chapter 15

the yeti

I was the first of the Chelsea players to find out that Ruud Gullit had been chosen to take over from Glenn Hoddle and was going to be the new manager. It was the end-of-season night out for the players and before it all the talk and the gossip had been about one subject – who the new boss was going to be. We were all due to go to a club in Windsor called Harpoon Louis's but, before we went, Ruud said to me that he was going for something to eat and he wanted me to join him.

I had become a good friend of Ruud's since he came to the club and we would spend a lot of time together on the golf course. We got on really well and I was quite close to him. Perhaps that's why he confided in me before he told anyone else. The two of us went to a Chinese restaurant.

'What's happening?' I asked Ruud. 'I am going to be manager next season. The club have asked me and I said I would take it.' Ruud replied. 'Good,' I said, 'I think that's a great idea'.

And I meant it. He knew the players, there was nothing you could teach him about football and he was fiercely ambitious. As far as I was concerned, it was a great decision. But I also think that he found it hard from that day on in many ways because, as a manager, you have to separate yourself from the players. You can't be too close as we found out under Ian Porterfield.

When he came to the club as a player the season before, he had blended in straight away, no problem. He had come with such a huge reputation that at first everyone was in awe of him. We didn't quite know what to expect. I mean we are talking about the definitive legend in the game; there wasn't too much he hadn't achieved. He had charisma. That is the only word for it. He was at ease immediately and joined in everything. He was so relaxed and it was a surprise – a pleasant one – that he was so down-to-earth. And he had a great sense of humour.

After one of the first training sessions with us he was walking down the corridor after getting out of the shower and he suddenly dropped the towel and bent over. 'Hey Wisey,' he shouted, 'have a look in the mirror.' Everyone cracked up and he showed that he was just one of the lads who enjoyed a joke as much as the next man. No one expected him to be like that. I think we all felt he would be a bit aloof, a bit above the rest of us, but he was nothing like that. He was one of us from day one. But that changed when he became manager, as it had to. Suddenly he was the boss and he couldn't be one of the crowd any more, he couldn't joke with the players like he used to and I think he missed that. Now it was up to him who played, who didn't, who was bought and who was sold. He had to tell players they were not wanted and I don't think that came easily to him – especially if they were friends of his.

The perfect example was John Spencer, our little Scottish striker. Ruud fell out with Spenny, who wanted to leave because he wasn't getting any first-team football and felt really frustrated about that. Ruud genuinely liked him and wanted to keep him at Chelsea, he wanted him to stay part of the set-up even though he wasn't going to play him all that often. It was an awkward situation and Ruud struggled to come to terms with it.

At times maybe he separated himself a bit too much. It is not as difficult if you go from one club to another but, when you are already mates with many of the squad, that can be a problem – particularly if you have to tell one that he is no longer needed at the club. But Ruud knew what he was taking on and there was no doubting that he was a big personality – a big man in the club and around the club.

He showed early on that he could take a joke – I was always calling him either Big Nose or the Yeti – and he was only too willing to mix it verbally with the lads. We lent him this book on Cockney slang, like we have done to all the foreign players. I was just sitting there with Kevin Hitchcock and suddenly he said, 'Hey, I am a gravedigger [slang for black] and I am a very rich gravedigger as well!' He knew exactly what he was saying and Hitch and me just cracked up. He wasn't bothered about things like that and was only too willing to join in the dressing-room banter.

That changed quite a lot when he took over from Hoddle. To start with, there was his method of telling you the team – or rather letting you read the team. Initially, it got to him when he had to drop people but he came to terms with that and eventually the routine was introduced that never altered from then until the day he left. At 1.30 on a Saturday afternoon or at 6.15 on a weekday he would come in and pin up the team sheet. He didn't give an explanation. Everyone would be standing around but no one dared get changed because you couldn't second-guess that you were in the team. Of course players prefer to know the day before if they are playing but the good thing about this method was that everyone was kept on their toes. But players prefer to be told in person and I fell out with him once about that system.

On a Saturday morning before we played Wimbledon at home in a league game I read in one of the papers that I was going to be dropped. Confirmation came when the team sheet went up. I was on the bench and I wasn't happy. 'Anyone got anything to say?' he asked. I said, 'Yes, I have. How come I have to find out from a newspaper that I am not playing?' Ruud said it wasn't something that should be discussed in front of everyone but I said I wasn't fussed if we did talk about it. He said, 'I haven't spoken to the papers, they just guessed.' In the end I accepted what he said.

The result of that fracas was I didn't play for the next two or three matches and I began to wonder if Ruud really fancied me as a player and if he really wanted me to stay at Chelsea. The relationship between us became a bit strained and he spoke to my mate Jim Creed to ask if everything was alright with me and whether I had a problem with him. Jim advised me to give him a call and to go round and see him to clear the air. I rang him and he said without hesitation that I should go round. We spoke about things at Chelsea and he told me what he wanted and then asked what I wanted. I said I wanted a new contract. He had given one to Steve Clarke and a couple of other players and I wanted that reassurance that he wanted me to stay at the club as well.

All players, no matter who they are, welcome that kind of confidence boost and that is why I think Arsène Wenger is a good manager. When he took over at Arsenal one of the first things he did was to give new deals to Tony Adams, Lee Dixon, Steve Bould and Nigel Winterburn. It was proof that he rated them, valued them and wanted them to stay. I wanted a similar gesture from my new manager and, to be fair, I got it.

I did have another run-in with Ruud, the following season. I had been playing with a toe injury that required me to take eight tablets a day but I was getting through the games alright. For the league game at Goodison Park he wanted to put me on the bench. He said it was because of my toe problem. I wasn't happy with that and was annoyed that he was planning to bring Eddie Newton back even though he had had just a week's training after injury. 'I can still play,' I said. But he insisted Eddie would play. I then said, 'If you are going to rest me, then rest me completely, don't put me on for 15 or 20 minutes when I could do more damage to the toe.' So he rested me.

Then, for the next game, against Arsenal in the first leg of the League Cup semi-final, he didn't even put me on the bench. I was out of the picture completely and I suppose it was his way of making a point. He clearly had the right hump with me about the business at Everton.

I think the team selection was the most difficult part of the job for Ruud, particularly when it came to picking himself. For a start you get a much better and broader view of the game when you are watching than when you are playing. It takes its toll on you and it must have been hard for him. As he settled into the job he became more ruthless with his decision-making.

In match preparation Ruud was very different from anyone else I had worked with at Chelsea. His team talks were very laid back. He would never worry about the opposition and all he would say is play your football, 'work hard and enjoy yourselves'. That, in essence, was his message. Everyone certainly went out in a positive frame of mind.

As far as the day-to-day running of the club went, it was Graham Rix who took most of the training. Ruud would sometimes join in and on other occasions would watch from the touchline. We had gone into Ruud's first season on the back of an enjoyable pre-season. It wasn't nearly as hard as everyone thought it was going to be. He was very laid back about training and didn't think it was a great idea to train too hard. We didn't argue.

If he had a fault, it was that he needed to make us more disciplined at set pieces. I lost count of the number of times that we would play wonderful football and deserve to win only to be undone by a set-piece goal from the opposition. I felt we needed to sort that part out but that area of the game just wasn't part of his thinking. He just told the defenders to mark certain players or certain zones. He was very relaxed and enjoyed it all and certainly didn't seem to feel the pressure. The approach was less tense than what we had experienced in the past.

After a game he would never really get mad but he would make sure he made his point. It was rare for Ruud to lose his temper. But there was one occasion when he lost it on the pitch and, in my mind, it was a big mistake. We were playing Tottenham in October 1996 in a Premiership match at Stamford Bridge. It was the Saturday after the death of Matthew Harding. Kevin Hitchcock was in goal and he made a real hash of a cross and ended up knocking the ball into his own net. Ruud, who was playing that day, was steaming. He tore down the field, picked the ball up, pointed at Hitch and then kicked the ball into the net. It was a gesture of real arrogance and for a while it really got to Hitch. His confidence was in tatters. Everyone saw it – the rest of the team and the fans – and Hitch was so, so nervous after that. I went to see Ruud about it because I just didn't think it was the right thing to do and I wanted him to know the effect it had on Hitch.

The angriest I have ever seen him at a match had nothing to do with us – but with the conditions in which we were asked to play. It was during the 1997-98 season and we were playing in Norway against Tromso in the European Cup Winners' Cup. The snow was relentless, it just never stopped and they had to keep holding up play to clear the lines and the pitch. We were losing 2-0 and Ruud wanted the game called off. He was steaming and, when the referee kept the game going, he stormed down the touchline in a real mood and kicked a lump of snow. Except it wasn't a lump of snow at all – it was a brick covered in snow and he broke his toe. It was so funny . . . to everyone but Ruud, of course. Poor bloke, it must have been so embarrassing for him.

But I have never seen him go mad in the dressing room afterwards and start throwing cups or anything like that. He would make his point with his presence and you knew when he was upset. But I wouldn't say he was a person to carry it on and on for days. He wasn't one to hold a grudge.

Everyone thought that doing two jobs would be a really taxing exercise and that is how it turned out. Was he less happy than when he was just a player? Well, he was certainly different. I think deep down he would rather have been one of the lads. While at Chelsea he had that huge psychological thing about deciding whether or not it was time to hang his boots up. Deep down, I felt, he thought he could still do a good job out there on the field. But the pressures on a manager are different. He went to Newcastle, of course, purely and simply as a manager, and I think he was better off for it.

Chapter 16

the foreign legion arrives

During the summer of 1996 Ruud made some crucial signings: Gianluca Vialli, Frank Leboeuf and Roberto di Matteo. As a player who had joined Chelsea when they were struggling to make an impact, I welcomed the arrival of these stars. You could see from the moment they joined that they were quality players. The rest of the lads were very impressed. I had been part of the Chelsea scene for six years and, when I saw people of their ability arrive at the club, I began to think that I might have cracked it. They were all players who had been successful at other clubs, and people like that tend to bring success with them. I was all for it. It seemed that no matter where they went something good happened.

Some people outside the club were convinced that there would be resentment from the players already there to the influx of all these foreign players. Nothing could have been further from the truth. You do get it but, in our case, definitely not. It doesn't matter to me what people are earning – if they produce it on the field, then fair enough. You don't argue with that . . . or with what those three players brought to the club. That kind of policy doesn't always pay off and you only have to look at what happened to Middlesbrough that same season as proof. I haven't a clue what went wrong up there, not after they brought in Juninho and Fabrizio Ravanelli who were bigger names than our signings. Obviously the balance was wrong because they got relegated.

But the players we got had the opposite effect – they were a great mix. They got on well with each other and with the rest of the lads. They joined in the banter and they all liked a joke. They immediately added to the team spirit at the club. The players already there could see they were good people as well as good players and things just carried on as normal, if not better. There were no little groups or cliques; in fact there were more of them when I first came to the club when British players dominated the squad.

The new lads were accepted without hesitation. You saw them do things in training or in a match and you thought, 'Bloody hell, he is one good player.' It didn't matter what nationality they were. With good players you get success and we all wanted that.

Naturally, as the foreign lads tried to pick up the language, we did our best to put them wrong by telling them wrong phrases. Someone like Luca would say, 'How do you say "Thank You" in a phrase?' Luca loved his phrases. We'd say, 'What you say, Luca, is "Thank you hairy crutch".' Then he would say it and we would all stop ourselves laughing because we wanted him to use the phrase in everyday situations once he was away from Stamford Bridge. Another time Luca wanted to say, 'When the chips are down', and someone told him that the right phrase is 'When the fish is on the table'.

We did something similar with Frank Leboeuf. He claims to this day that he didn't say it but I can assure you he did. He wanted the word to say that his boots were excellent and gave him no problems. 'What do you say . . . ?' 'Convertible,' I said to him. 'Oh,' he said. 'So, yes, my boots are very convertible.' I said that was perfect and the rest of the lads creased up when he started saying it. Now their English is wonderful; in fact it's better than mine, although some might say that isn't difficult. Except that is for Franco Zola, who came a few months later. He still struggles a bit and gets a lot of stick for it.

It has all gone to prove that not only are these players great footballers but also very intelligent men. They have adjusted and adapted well. And we did our best to make them feel welcome. When Luca first came over, I immediately got on well with him. We would go out for a meal and go to the pictures. Even so, it was easier for him when the others arrived. It meant no one was on his own.

They also took to our habits, after some initial surprises. Soon after Franco joined he found out what it meant to go to an English club's Christmas party. Franco doesn't drink but that didn't mean anything to big Erland Johnsen. 'Come here you midget!' he ordered after a few beers and he grabbed Franco round the neck and held his head tight. Poor Franco couldn't move. Then Erland ordered two large brandies and insisted that Franco drink one – which he did. You could see by his face that he found it disgusting but he was so scared of Erland that he wasn't going to argue. I think he was frightened that Erland would rip his head off. 'You see,' Ruud said to Franco, 'You can't believe this can you? All this lot, they are mad.' You could see Franco looking round, more than a bit dazed and his eyes said everything. 'What am I doing here?' they seemed to say.

They all agreed that it was different from Italy. Over here all the lads show their togetherness and go out as a group to have a laugh. And, believe me, the foreign lads love it. It takes them a bit of time at first to relax and feel at ease but now they feel very much part of the scene and very at home.

But in any environment where you have big personalities and big players you are going to get friction and there was something of a problem between Luca and Ruud. It started soon after we signed Gianfranco Zola from Parma at the beginning of November 1996. We could see from the start that Franco was a class act. The problem – if you could call it that because I am sure it is a situation that many managers would welcome – was that we now had three excellent strikers for two places. In training we tried using all of them in a 4-3-3 formation but it just didn't seem right for Ruud, so he scrapped it. Ruud had to choose between Franco, Luca and Hughesie. He went for Franco and Hughesie and that left Luca out in the cold.

It wasn't a situation to which Luca was accustomed and he clearly wasn't happy about it. To put it bluntly, he became really pissed off about it. It was hard for him because, basically, he had done nothing wrong. He had scored goals and the fans had taken to him straight away. His goal ratio was one every two games – and any striker would tell you he would be happy with that. But for some reason Ruud went for the other two as a partnership, and as a result Ruud and Luca hardly spoke to each other.

I remember one incident when we were playing Arsenal in the League Cup the following season and Luca still wasn't a regular. I know for a fact he was fed up and disillusioned with everything that was happening. In the last minutes of the game Ruud said, 'Get changed, Luca. You're going on.' Luca turned to the rest of us on the bench and said, 'Do I deserve this? Is that all I am worth now – two minutes?' and started laughing.

Luca had become very popular among the players; we all loved him. We could see he was suffering and wanted to do something to cheer him up. So Roberto di Matteo and I decided to show him what he meant to us. It was January 1997 and we were playing Derby at Stamford Bridge. Underneath our Chelsea shirts we had T-shirts with 'Cheer up Luca, we all love you' written on them. We decided that, if one of us scored, we'd lift up our Chelsea shirt during the celebration and show the message.

It is so funny how things work out, it really is. I hardly ever score but that day I did. I ran over to the bench where Luca was sitting with my club shirt pulled up and the message revealed. Luca just burst out laughing. He loved it and he really knew what the rest of us thought about him as a person and a player.

Luca was fit enough to play – there was no doubt about that – and, when he did play, he usually scored. His average was remarkable. A personality clash with Ruud? I don't know for sure but there might well have been. You have to remember these were two strong people. What happened between them I don't know but certainly they hardly talked to each other. It was a very difficult situation. Luca just wanted to play and Ruud wouldn't pick him – it was as simple as that. Luca didn't want to stop playing or anything like that but, although he generally worked hard in training, there were times when the whole situation seemed to get to him and he didn't work as hard as he should have done. But 90 per cent of the time he worked his nuts off.

Ruud would use him when he thought he had to and that was the case when we played Leicester in the league up at Filbert Street in October 1996. Luca had started on the bench and Mark Nicholls, a young player still learning his craft, was preferred up front. It was also a game after which I was left fuming. At half-time we were 1-0 down and not doing too well at all. Ruud decided it was time for Luca to come on and he replaced Mark Nicholls. He also took me off and I was steaming about that. But you couldn't argue with the final result – we won 3-1 and Luca was brilliant when he came on. He swung the game for us and scored a goal. It proved once again that, when Luca played, he scored.

Chapter 17

tragedy and triumph

That season, 1996-97, Chelsea had a tragic loss.

We came back late after losing at Bolton in the Coca-Cola Cup and, when we got to Stamford Bridge, Ruud came up to me and said he had some very bad news. 'There has been an accident,' he said. 'A helicopter has crashed and I may have to tell the players tomorrow that the vice-chairman Matthew Harding has died in that crash. We are not quite sure yet but we think it may be him who is involved.'

The following day it was confirmed: Matthew Harding had been killed. It was a huge shock and there was talk of asking the Premiership to call off the next league game, against Tottenham at Stamford Bridge. But it was decided that the match should go ahead and on reflection that was the right decision. It was a terrible shock and a tragic loss of a man who was a Chelsea fanatic. But we would have had to play sooner or later and it was better that we just got on with life at Stamford Bridge. Before the match on the following Saturday it was decided among the players that we would show our respect by taking a huge wreath out on to the pitch and having a minute's silence. We also thought it would be fitting if, rather than stand around the centre-circle, we would face the Matthew Harding Stand. It was an emotional start to a game, very different and very strange. It was almost an unreal atmosphere and we had somehow to put all that to the back of our minds as soon as the match started. We did and we won 3-1.

The players had been aware of the boardroom battle between Harding and Bates over who would control the club. Ken Bates was chairman and Matthew Harding wanted to be. But, to be honest, none of the players were too fussed about it. It was nothing to do with us. There is no way I will speak ill of anyone who is in no position to speak for themselves but personally I am a Ken Bates man – I always have been and I always will be. From the first time I met him, when I joined from Wimbledon, we got on well. We are similar people in many ways. With me, what you see is what you get and it is the same with Ken Bates. I am pleased he kept control of the club because he has always had the club at heart. When he took over in 1982 the club were going nowhere and had debts of £1 million. That was a lot of money then. He has been largely responsible for turning it around.

There seemed to be people looking elsewhere at people like Matthew Harding to take his place and, for me, they shouldn't have done that. To put it bluntly, Ken Bates is the man who got Chelsea out of the mire and in the last five years he has ploughed money into the club – both on the squad and on the stadium. That is the kind of man you want in charge. We now have a wonderful stadium and a wonderful team and an awful lot of that is down to Batesy. I think he learned from that situation when others were trying to get him out – and a lot of people outside, they have learned as well. They have learned Ken Bates is a very difficult opponent.

But, all that aside, Matthew's death was a tragedy for everyone concerned, his family, the club, the players and the supporters. But we just had to knuckle down and get on with our football. After all, Matthew was a Chelsea fan and that is what he would have wanted.

There were setbacks that season on the pitch too – like the time we lost 5-1 up at Liverpool when Luca was on the receiving end of some fearful verbal stick from the crowd and one or two Liverpool players because of his bald head. But the lowest we ever dropped to was eighth in the table and that was about as high as I had previously been while at Chelsea. It seemed since I joined we had always been in the bottom half, always looking to make sure we stayed out of the relegation area, but now there was a new belief. Now we stayed up the business end of the league and that was down to the new players, no question. We knew we were a top-half side and the targets changed from previous years. Now the aim was the top six and then top five. We felt we were good enough and you could feel the change in the place. There was a great buzz, a good confident feel after all those years of frustration.

Although we felt the league title might have been beyond us still, there was a genuine feeling we might do well in the FA Cup. Of course, you are dependent on good draws. They are essential. And you need that bit of luck. But we felt we could do it. The FA Cup was also a new experience for the new lads like Frank Leboeuf, Franco, Roberto di Matteo and Luca. They couldn't really appreciate what it meant to the players and the supporters until they played in it. Then they knew alright.

It soon became clear how much they wanted to play at Wembley in front of a full house. Franco had known what it was like playing there for Italy; in February 1997 he had scored the winning goal in a World Cup qualifier against England. He wanted to go back after that. He was quite funny the day after that game. He came in to the training ground for a warm down with Roberto di Matteo, who had also played. They came out on to the pitch with their arms round each other wearing the biggest grins you had ever seen – plus their Italy tracksuits. They didn't say anything, they didn't need to. The night before at Wembley they had shoved it right up us.

But they did get a warm greeting from one player – Mark Hughes. Hughesie is Welsh and there is nothing the Welsh, Irish and Scots like better than to see England beaten at anything. Hughesie nearly broke Franco in half with the hug he gave him that morning. We got our own back, though, the following October when England drew in Rome to reach the World Cup finals as group winners. They got some stick when we all met up again at the club, even though neither of them played in the second game.

Back to the cup and the need for kind draws. It started well enough for us with a tie in the third round against West Bromwich Albion. With respect to them it was comfortable enough. But then came the turning point of our season in the fourth round: Liverpool at home. If you are going to get a big side, get them on your own patch is what they say and we were up for it against a team who had beaten us so convincingly at Anfield earlier in the season.

After 45 minutes we were 2-0 down and it could have been even worse. They had a great chance to make it 3-0; Steve McManaman missed an absolute sitter. If he had scored, that would have been curtains. There would have been no comeback from there.

During the first half I had had a run-in with John Barnes, more of a pushing and shoving match than anything else. Anyway, walking off at half-time, he turned round to Robbie Fowler and said, 'This is easy, no problem.' He wasn't saying that at the end.

Ruud had started with Luca and Franco. It was like Luca was being told, 'Show us what you can do. Away you go.' But we had made little progress. At half-time we just had to change things. It was all-or-nothing time and Ruud reacted. He decided to bring on Hughesie, a real competitor who gave us a physical edge up front that Liverpool clearly didn't like. He also told Roberto di Matteo to push forward more as we tried to retrieve the game with a 3-3-1-3 formation. 'We have to go for it or else we are out,' Ruud said. And we came good with a fabulous comeback. Hughesie scored the first, Luca scored two and Franco got another as we won 4-2. At half-time we thought the season might be over. Suddenly it was very much alive.

The next round saw us up at Leicester. Franco got a bit of a roasting from their fans because it was his first game after scoring the winner for Italy against England, but he coped alright and we should have gone through on the day, no problem. We were 2-0 up and the sixth round was in our sights but then we let in two really sloppy goals. First, Frank Sinclair gave away an unnecessary free-kick near our penalty area which was something we talked about before the game. We didn't want Leicester to have the ammunition for their big players like Steve Walsh, Matt Elliott and Spencer Prior. Walsh duly scored and suddenly they had hope. And in the last minute they equalised from another free-kick near our box. This time Eddie Newton touched the ball into his own net.

So it was back to Stamford Bridge for the replay and a night of real controversy. We were given a penalty in extra-time when Erland Johnsen went down in their area and all hell broke loose. Fingers were pointed and Prior was calling Erland a cheat although I have to say from where I was on the pitch it did look like a penalty. Okay, I admit when I saw it afterwards in slow motion it didn't but no one on the pitch has the benefit of that technology. It is alright for Andy Gray to sit up there in the Sky studio and say this and that with the help of his computer but decisions in football – by players and referees – are made on the spur of the moment. And that means mistakes can happen.

Back in the penalty area there was a real mêlée, a lot of arguments and I got really involved with Steve Walsh. When calm was restored, Frank Leboeuf scored and I was then right out of order. I ran up to Walsh and gave him a real mouthful. As I went back to get ready for the kick-off, I felt really bad about what I had done. I actually went back and apologised. 'Walshie, I am sorry I said that,' I said. And I meant it. You do and say things in tense situations and this had been a real nitty-gritty game in which Leicester had made it really hard for us. It seemed to me they came to play for penalties and it nearly worked. Anyway we were through and now it was Portsmouth away in the quarter-finals.

Fratton Park has never been an easy place to go to, especially when there's a big crowd in. And at this time they had Terry Venables in charge, and you know what I think of him. He is top class and there was no doubt they would be highly motivated and ready for us. There was even talk of him having a master-plan to beat us and that this would be the game where the foreign softies at Chelsea would be exposed.

All I know is we were really tuned in for that game and Mark Hughes, in particular, was magnificent. Portsmouth just couldn't handle him or, indeed, the rest of us. By that stage of the competition we all realised that a lot of good teams had gone out and we were looking one of the better teams left in. This could be our year after all. Even I scored twice in a 4-1 win that day. Steve Clarke has not forgiven me for one of those goals, though. His shot looked as if it would trickle over the line and, from about an inch out, I put it in. 'I'm sorry Clarkey,' I said afterwards, 'but I had to make sure.' That would have been his first goal for years. But he forgave me, just.

So we were in the last four along with Middlesbrough, Chesterfield and Wimbledon, and we were paired with my old club for a clash at Highbury. In all honesty, it was probably a good time to play Wimbledon. Not long before our match they had gone out of the Coca-Cola Cup in the semi-final against Leicester after looking certainties to go through. They had drawn 0-0 at Filbert Street and Marcus Gayle had put them ahead in the second leg. They must have felt they were going back to Wembley but in the second half Simon Grayson equalised and that put the tie into extra-time. Even then they had chances but Garry Parker cleared off the line and they were out on the away-goals rule. They must have felt devastated because they really fancied their chances of winning that competition and it takes a long time to get over that feeling, believe me, I know.

That defeat killed them. I sensed when we arrived at Highbury that day that we had the edge. I saw their manager Joe Kinnear before the game and said, 'It's not your day you know.' He just laughed a bit nervously. You sensed they were a bit worried and that came over when I was speaking to Vinnie before the game. He just sounded worried. I think deep down they knew they couldn't beat us.

A lot of people thought that Ruud played things totally off the cuff but tactically he was very aware and often very shrewd. He thought long and hard about how we would play against Wimbledon. A key man was going to be Roberto di Matteo. Ruud wanted him to play up against Vinnie Jones and make a lot of runs because Roberto was a lot quicker than Vinnie and he felt this would give Wimbledon problems. Ruud reckoned that Roberto could easily lose him and that would give us an extra dimension and added advantage.

We also worked hard on getting players overlapping to stop Wimbledon catching us offside. They move up quickly and teams struggle to stay on side against them but we worked and worked on our strategy and it paid off with the first goal. The ball was played up to Franco and I overlapped him and he played me in. With a fair bit of space I put in an early cross that caused confusion. The ball rebounded off Alan Kimble and Mark Hughes put us ahead.

We also had a plan to cope with Wimbledon's famous aggression. After two minutes Neil Ardley fouled me and we decided beforehand that the first time something like that happened we would all get round the referee and make a point. Basically we wanted them booked and it worked. Neil was booked. It wasn't very nice but we wanted to draw Wimbledon's physical sting. Neil then had to play 88 minutes being very careful about every challenge. They wanted to get stuck in and we wanted them to be wary of doing that. The plan worked a treat.

We played really well on what turned out to be a wonderful day – with a wonderful second goal from Franco. He was on fire that day on a terrific surface at Highbury and the goal summed up his performance. He got possession at the edge of the area and did a 'Johan' – in other words, a Cruyff drag-back. Dean Blackwell and Chris Perry were taken out of the game completely by Franco's turn – and then he smacked the ball home. That was it. All over. Not even Wimbledon were going to come back from that. Hughesie added a third in the last minute and the celebrations began.

I can even remember seeing pictures on the television of Ruud jumping up in the air and punching out in joy. None of us had ever seen him react like that before. Never. Ruud and Luca even cuddled each other on the touchline and Luca got some fearful stick about that. 'That's your daddy,' we said. 'Luca has found his daddy.'

I did feel for Vinnie after the game. It was the second semi-final he had lost in a matter of weeks and you just knew this was going to be his last chance of going back to Wembley. But, honestly, there cannot be any room for sentiment in this game and, for all that I felt for him, I was delighted for us.

After the match we went back to the hotel and watched the Middlesbrough v Chesterfield game. Obviously we wanted Chesterfield to win. Ask any Premiership club and they would always rather play a cup match against a lower division team, especially on a neutral ground. Chesterfield should have won as well and, when their perfectly good goal after the ball hit the bar and went over the line was ruled out, a lot of abuse and rubbish was thrown at the television by the Chelsea players. The match was drawn and Middlesbrough went on to win the replay. Even so we felt – no, we were convinced – we had the players to get our previous appearance in the final, against Manchester United, out of our system.

I had a major scare in the build-up to the final. At one time, I was genuinely afraid that I would miss it. I tore a stomach muscle right near the groin and a specialist said I would need an operation. But I was determined to play and a man called Ted Troost played a big part in getting me to Wembley. Ruud had introduced him to the club and he came in once a week to help with the muscles. He knew how to relax them – although his methods were less than pleasant. He was 6 foot 2 inches tall, weighed about 16 stone and was built like a brick outhouse. He would sit on your back and make it go into spasms. It was amazing what he could do because he made the muscles very supple. I could never stretch my groin before working with him but I could once he did his stuff. It hurt at first. In fact it hurt a lot. But before long I could put my groin at 90 degrees and it was totally relaxed. Once you get through the pain, you are fine. It is amazing how you can stretch your body and he helped me a lot.

I missed five league games in all but managed to play in the last couple of games before the final, which I had to do to prove to Ruud I was fit to play in it. I was panicking because I wanted to play so, so badly and I was petrified I would miss out. I will admit to being selfish and say that if I could have played for five minutes and then come off, I would have been happy. Just as long as I could go up and collect the FA Cup at the end. I just knew deep down that we would win.

On the day of the final I did some work with Ted and I was okay. I was in a bit of pain but I was alright to play. But one man who wasn't involved was Craig Burley and he was bitterly upset. He had been involved in most of the cup matches and had played a key role for us in the semi-final win over Wimbledon. But at Wembley, he wasn't even on the bench. He was shattered. Only Craig and Ruud know the real reason for him being left out like that. It seems there was some kind of contract issue – Ruud wanted Craig to sign a new deal before the final, Craig wanted to wait until afterwards. Craig was left out and whether his delay in signing the contract had anything to do with it, I don't know.

What I do know is that Ruud likes to get his own way. He is a strong man and he will not budge until he gets what he wants. He will make a decision and, if he wants to do something, he will do it. In a strange way it was when he adopted that more ruthless approach that he became a better manager. If he felt the need to take a particular course of action, if he knew what he had to do, then he would just carry on and, if someone's feelings got hurt in the process, so be it.

During that season, he had gradually become more distant from the players. Yes, he would still like a joke but there was no socialising or anything like that. That had to come to an end and it did. You can't have players going out and having a beer with the manager on a regular basis, that just doesn't work. Not even as a friend. The manager has difficult enough decisions to make and they would be even harder if a friend at the club was involved. It was almost impossible to argue with Ruud. Or rather, you could argue but he had his point to make and he had the last say. You saw that with first Luca and then Craig.

On the day of the final I had this wonderful feeling that we were going to win, that a trophy was coming to Chelsea for the first time in a quarter of a century. There is no doubt in my mind that we were well prepared for the game. Of course you get the odd bout of nerves. I remember saying to Steve Clarke, 'We have got to win this, we have to.' It was the only way we were going to shut people up about the seventies and how great it had been then. That was being thrown at us all the time and I just wanted, as Chelsea captain, to walk up those steps and say, 'Right, now talk about the team of the nineties.'

The first time I was at Wembley, for the 1988 FA Cup final, was extraordinary. That wall of sound, the noise when you walk out, everything about the day is so, so memorable. You can never replicate that experience, no matter how many times you go back. What it does do, though, is whet your appetite for success. Once you have been there, you want more of the same. You can never get tired of playing at Wembley in cup finals. I just remember thinking after that first final with Wimbledon, 'I want more of this. This is something I want to get used to.' The occasion never changes and to go up and collect a trophy as the winning captain is still one of the most memorable moments that a player can have in his career.

It took just 43 seconds for us to know it was our cup. We were all aware of what Middlesbrough had been through that season – losing the League Cup final to Leicester and then, despite having Ravanelli, Juninho and Emerson, being relegated. The early goal from Roberto di Matteo just about killed them off. If they felt a bit down coming into the game, now they were reeling. Then Ravanelli went off and everything was going for us. Now the foreign lads, the Leboeufs, Zolas, Viallis and di Matteos knew what the FA Cup was about. They had revelled in the build-up, all the things that go with the FA Cup. Now they were tasting the real thing. With four minutes to go Eddie Newton got the second and that was it.

At the final whistle it was pure elation. Everything flashed through my mind – the noise, the crowd, the colour, Europe (and this time with a much better team not restricted by the 'foreigners' rule). As I was going round with the cup, I went into the crowd and pulled out a kid of about ten. His dad couldn't believe it but the kid had his full Chelsea kit on and I wanted him to know what Wembley was like, I wanted him to know what the pitch was like, what it is like to be among winners in the team he supported. I took him down the dressing room and then Gwyn Williams came in and said his dad was at the big gates at the top of the tunnel to collect his son. He came back and said all the father could say was 'Thank you, thank you, thank you'. And that he was crying his eyes out. That's when you know what football means to people.

I knew what it meant to Ken Bates, too. He had taken on a huge job back in 1982 but had rebuilt the club on and off the pitch. Now he had success at last after all those years of trying.

From Wembley we went to the Waldorf – and it was there that I claimed some Wembley glory for myself. Roberto's goal was fantastic, one of the best as well as the quickest ever at Wembley in an FA Cup final. I always claimed an assist because I was the one who gave him the ball, although I have to admit it was well inside our own half at the time. At the Wardolf, I was standing with Roberto's family, including his sister Conchi, who is blind. I said to her, 'Conchi, shall I describe Roberto's goal to you?' 'Yes,' she replied. 'Well,' I explained, 'I took the ball past two Middlesbrough players, then pushed the ball through the legs of another and then round two more. I ran into the penalty area, drew the goalkeeper, went round him and stopped the ball an inch from the goal-line. Then I let Robbie come up and tap it over.' Roberto was with us and he and the family burst out laughing. And before anyone gets upset, Conchi did as well.

The following day, after a fantastic parade through Chelsea, we went off on a tour to the Far East. During the summer Craig Burley joined Celtic and I wish him all the success he deserves there. And me? I had one of the best summers ever. Not only had we won the FA Cup, we sensed there were better things ahead. After all those years of frustration, Chelsea were winners again and I knew, deep down, that this was just the start of something, not the end. Better things were coming. I just knew it.

Chapter 18

the bombshell

During the summer of 1997 I needed an operation to cure the stomach muscle injury that had bothered me going into the FA Cup final. I aggravated it at Wembley against Middlesbrough and I took advantage of the close season to get it right for the following campaign. It was a great summer. I recuperated from surgery and had my batteries charged up by the rest. Ruud Gullit, meanwhile, was busy in the transfer market. He wanted to make sure that we built on the FA Cup success and to the club came Gustavo Poyet, Ed de Goey, Celestine Babayaro, Graeme Le Saux and Bernard Lambourde. And later in the season we were to get the Norwegian striker Tore Andre Flo. It was clear that Ruud was ambitious. He wanted more silverware and I sensed even greater things were on the horizon.

Ed de Goey, the goalkeeper, proved to be a great signing. He came from Feyenoord and Ruud clearly knew all about him from his time in Holland. His judgment was spot on. If you come from a big club abroad as a goalkeeper, it can sometimes be a bit of a risk to go into our Premiership. At Feyenoord he probably had half a dozen difficult games a season playing football which isn't nearly as fast as the game in this country, with not nearly as much action around the goal. But Eddie adapted straightaway. He is a giant of a man and that is always reassuring to see in a goalkeeper. It gives him presence around the six-yard box and defenders feel comfortable with him around. It gives them confidence.

Mind you, he made a bit of a boob in his first home game against

131

Southampton when he was a victim of the rule that goalkeepers can't pick up a back-pass. When the ball came to him he hit it straight at Kevin Davies, who promptly tapped it past him into the net. But we won the game and, to be honest, that kind of thing can happen to any goalkeeper. We knew right away that in Ed de Goey we had a quality man as the last line of defence.

At the start of the season it was clear to me that Ruud thought we were more than capable of taking our challenge for honours a step further. It had been a long time since Chelsea had been regarded as a serious threat in the league. Cups, yes – Chelsea always seemed to do fairly well in those. But the league? No chance, too inconsistent. Ruud felt we were capable of taking that next big step. He felt we had the quality and quantity to make a big push for the first title since 1955. And, with six new players, there was certainly strength in depth.

This season, though, not everyone was delighted at the new arrivals – like the younger players in the first-team squad and the reserves, like Jody Morris. It was difficult for them and Jody, in particular, seemed to go off the boil a bit. Of course you are going to get disillusioned when you are not playing all the time. That's only natural. But the youngsters have to keep in mind that Chelsea is a big club and big clubs sign big players. They have to remember that there is still going to be room and opportunity for home-grown talent – and the old maxim still holds good: if you are good enough, you are going to play. They have to be patient, that is essential.

Jody is one of a very good crop of young players at the club – possibly the best prospect Chelsea have ever had – but sometimes that season his attitude didn't do him any favours. At the cup final banquet I really had a go at him, telling him some home truths. I said that if he didn't buck his ideas up he'd end up playing pub football. What I said really upset him. I didn't want to hurt him because I think a lot of him as a person and as a player but I was being cruel to be kind. It was important for him to remember that there aren't too many bigger clubs that the young players can go to. Basically, after a top club like Chelsea, it's downhill all the way. Of course, it can be the same at other clubs. I mean, look at my mate Vaughan Ryan at Wimbledon. He was a tenacious little midfield player but he got so cheesed off with not getting a regular chance in the first team he decided to leave. Leyton Orient came in for him, offered him a pay rise and he decided to accept. I could never understand why he did that. Why would anyone choose to drop down from the top division to one of the lower leagues? I asked him why he chose to leave and he said because he would be playing all the time. I said in time he would get that at Wimbledon but he was determined to move. What happened? He was injured and then drifted out of football. I think he knows he made a mistake in leaving Wimbledon because I am sure he would have come through in the end. The plan of action for a young player should always be to start lower down – play for a smaller club or in the reserves at a big club – and then work your way up. You don't start high and then go down. Go out on loan by all means but don't quit because you can't be bothered to fight for your place. The danger at times is that the kids think they have cracked it when they sign for Chelsea and they get complacent with a 'I have made it already' kind of attitude. I was a bit like that in my early days at Southampton and I learned my lesson. Jody has been much better recently and now he is very much part of the first-team squad and, on many occasions, the team. He has stuck at it and come through and I am delighted for him. He is an example to the other young players of what can be achieved through effort and discipline.

We had to play our first three games of the season away from home because of building work at Stamford Bridge. The first was Coventry away, and for some reason we always struggle to get a result there. We dominated the match – in fact every time we play them at Highfield Road we seem to dominate the match – but we just couldn't win. It was the same that day. We were beaten 3-2 and each one of their goals was a sloppy one. We were done on three set pieces and it was all so disappointing because we really wanted a good start to the league programme. We were cruising at one stage and then we blew it.

In the next match, against Barnsley, we proved what we could do in pretty spectacular fashion. We won 6-0. Luca played brilliantly that day and scored four goals. We were all so delighted for him after what he had suffered the previous season and the result and the performance frightened the life out of a few people.

The atmosphere between Luca and Ruud was still tense and they still didn't have much to say to each other. We felt for Luca at the FA Cup final when he only came on for the last two minutes and was clearly very fed up with things. But he is an excellent professional and kept himself really sharp to take full advantage of the openings when they came along. And he certainly did that at Barnsley. He was lethal.

A 2-0 win at Wimbledon and a 4-2 win at home to Southampton followed. Then we won 3-0 at Crystal Palace to go into third place in the league. There was a real feeling about the place that we could build on the previous season when we made that huge breakthrough in winning the FA Cup. We had played five league games and four of them had been away. We were right up there and we were ready for our biggest test of the season to date – a home game with Arsenal. This was going to tell us what progress we had made.

We went 1-0 up through Gus Poyet but then Frank Leboeuf was sent off. It was a huge turning point. It is always going to be difficult against a team of Arsenal's ability when you are a man short. It had been a highly competitive game with tackles flying all over the place. But you expect that in a London derby. Graeme Le Saux and Ray Parlour had a run-in and myself and Patrick Vieira got involved in a tussle, and he gave me a slap round the face. I was determined to get my own back and have to admit to doing a terrible tackle on him. The ball was there to be won when I went in on him and I won it. The problem was I took him as well and there was a big furore. When he stood up and glared at me I realised just how big he was. But these confrontations always happen in derby games.

Anyway, Arsenal got their own back on me with what turned out to be the winning goal. It should never have been allowed. The match was at 2-2 at the time and we would have settled for that with us being down to ten men. Then Arsenal started a move down their left and

Nigel Winterburn got the ball and closed in on our goal. I had seen the danger and was running over to block his run and he would not have shot if I had got there. But, thanks to Emmanuel Petit, I didn't get there. While all eyes were on Winterburn, Petit booted the back of my heel to bring me down and I went flying. No one saw it and Winterburn went on to fire the winner home with a great shot. We were fuming but no one had seen what had happened. We had lost and we all felt a bit deflated.

However, Ruud was still sure we could mount a title challenge. He was more confident and stronger now. He was very single-minded about things. The FA Cup win had given him more self-assurance and now that he was a proven winner as a manager he wanted to build on that. He didn't mess about in the transfer market and neither did the club. He identified the players he wanted and the club backed his judgment. He bought proven quality and added good players to what was an already strong group of players.

Within three days of the defeat against Arsenal, we went up to Manchester United and proved we had character. If you are feeling sorry for yourselves at a place like Old Trafford, you get hammered. But we were up for it and we were in no mood to let United walk all over us. We started really well and went a goal up when a shot from Graeme Le Saux ricocheted off Henning Berg and went over Peter Schmeichel into the net. Then they got an equaliser through Paul Scholes, which we felt was yards offside. Ruud was storming down the touchline arguing with the linesman but it made no difference – you don't get many decisions going your way as the away team at Old Trafford. That is something that hasn't changed over the years.

Then came a flare-up on the field that was to spill over into the tunnel and leave me with a cut eye. There was a row involving Roy Keane and Andy Myers, now of Bradford City, over in the corner and they ended up throwing punches at one another. As we were walking off at half-time Keane said to Andy, 'I'll do you in the tunnel.' He wanted it sorted out. I was walking behind them and heard what he said. 'Okay,' I said, 'I'll have some of that.' Andy was up for it as well.

When we got in the tunnel, Keane went for Andy and I went to go and help, punching Keane in the side of the head. Nicky Butt was behind me and he got involved and caught me just under the eye. A big scuffle broke out but it was over as soon as it started. Andy didn't come out worse, either. He is a big, strong lad who can handle himself. Nothing came of it all, no one saw anything and, to be honest, it is the type of thing that happens a lot in football.

In the second half we went 2-1 up and then Ole Gunnar Solskjaer equalised four minutes from the end with a bad goal from our point of view. There was a defensive mix-up and that was it: we'd lost two points when we should have won three. But perhaps just as important was the way that we proved to everyone – including ourselves – that we could recover from setbacks. So often when a team has a poor result, like ours against Arsenal, the rot sets in. That, I know, is what happened to Chelsea teams in the past. But not this one. We were made of stronger stuff.

One guy who was proving to be an enormous asset was Gus Poyet. He is close to being the complete midfield player: one who is strong, can take a challenge and not only scores goals but also sets them up for others. Unfortunately injury was to cut his season short and we particularly missed him in the league.

Poyet scored the winner in our next game against Newcastle but then came a setback at Liverpool. They had taken an early lead through Patrik Berger but Franco Zola equalised and we fancied getting something from a fixture that hadn't produced too many good results for us in the past. But Anfield, like Old Trafford, is a place where you don't get too many favours and that day we had Bernard Lambourde sent off. End of story. I can't think of too many teams that win with ten men. Yes, we got a penalty but it was all too late because we were 4-1 down at the time. That, from my experience, is when you start to get things at Anfield – when it is too late to matter.

We got back to winning ways against Leicester thanks to a thunderbolt from Frank Leboeuf and, although we lost to Bolton, we had hit a pretty consistent run and things started going for us. We won five of the next six and we were playing good stuff when we could and digging in when we had to get a result. We were always up there in third or fourth place. In fact, apart from the opening week, we were never lower than fifth all season.

We really came good as a strike force one week at the end of November and the beginning of December. First we beat Derby 4-0, then won 6-1 against Tottenham at White Hart Lane. Our fans really loved that one. Against Derby, Franco Zola was on fire. He scored a hat-trick and was unstoppable that day. A week later, it was Tore Andre Flo who scored three at Tottenham. The scoreline makes it look like a massacre but it was anything but that. We had seven chances that afternoon and scored six times and every bounce of the ball went our way. We couldn't seem to do anything wrong. They seemed to have just as many chances but scored only once. I think it was a case of confidence and good finishing.

Tottenham were going through a rough patch at the time and had just changed managers. Christian Gross had come from Zurich Grasshoppers a week or so before and in his first game came the result that always seems to come with a new manager – a win, up at Everton in Tottenham's case. But against us it was a very different story. Ed de Goey made some blinding saves that day and it was largely thanks to him that it was 1-1 at half-time. We got a lucky break early in the second half when a cross hit Roberto di Matteo and went in and Tottenham never seemed to recover. Every time we went forward that day we seemed to score.

I suppose it was inevitable really that after ten goals in two games we would draw a blank. We played Leeds at home and really needed to beat them to keep up our challenge for the title. We started the day in second place and badly wanted to keep our good run going. But really the referee spoiled it for us. It was a competitive game – they always are against Leeds because of the history between the two clubs that goes back to the 1970 FA Cup final – but never a dirty one. But they had two men sent off for offences that were really nothing more than petty. You assume that is going to give you a massive advantage but anyone in football will tell you it doesn't always work like that. They just packed their defence and left only one player upfield. On top of that Nigel Martyn in their goal had a magnificent game. He was unbeatable. I don't know what he was on that day . . . springs probably.

After the game, which ended 0-0, their players came off celebrating, really going potty. You would have thought they had won the FA Cup or something. In a way I couldn't blame them. They had done tremendously well to keep us out but I really fancied our chances of winning had the game been more open. It was another case of a referee not using common sense. I reckon about 90 per cent of them don't. They just stick to the guidelines and, as Gordon Strachan, the Coventry manager, once said, 'They know the rules but they don't know the game.' That was certainly true that day.

We recovered the goalscoring touch in the next game to win 4-1 at Sheffield Wednesday but could only draw with Wimbledon at home before losing at Southampton. Then came the match which many people thought afterwards was the beginning of the end for Ruud Gullit as manager – the first defence of the FA Cup, a third-round tie at home to Manchester United.

We were beaten 5-3 but the scoreline did us a favour because at one stage we were 5-0 down. It was an awful feeling, just awful. I was watching because of suspension and that just made it worse for me. I could do nothing to help. There were a few eyebrows raised when Ruud decided to put Mark Hughes in midfield. To be fair, we had lots of players missing for various reasons and we were particularly short in midfield. And it showed. United overran us and were on fire. There was nothing we could do and I reckon the way they were playing they could have beaten anyone. In the end we pulled back three late goals to make it look respectable but the truth was it was anything but that. We got back to winning ways against Coventry at home but then came the incident I mentioned earlier at Everton that was to prove such a problem between me and Ruud.

That day he also left Franco Zola out of the team. He said Franco was ill but I can assure you he wasn't and he wasn't happy that was the reason given out for him missing the game. On the day of the match the television cameras picked us up sitting up in the stand together watching the game and not looking at all pleased with life. A lot was made of that. We lost the game 3-1 and to many people that was a big shock. Everton weren't going well and we were expected to go up there and just collect the three points. It never works out like that, though.

For our next game, the away leg with Arsenal in the Coca-Cola Cup semi-final, I wasn't even substitute, although by then my foot had settled down. The Coca-Cola Cup had been a good competition for us that year. There had been some exciting games and, even though we had needed two penalty shoot-outs, against Blackburn and Ipswich, to reach the last four, we fancied we could do it over two legs against Arsenal. They had started off by playing what was virtually their reserve team in the earlier rounds but gradually brought in more established players as they made progress. And it was certainly a full-strength team that they had out for the first leg.

Ruud decided to play himself that night and, to be honest, he didn't do that well. He took a lot of stick and, although Arsenal were 2-0 up at one point, it could have been a lot, lot worse. They were all over us at times. Then late on we were given a lifeline when Mark Hughes scored from a Franco Zola cross. It kept us in with a great chance – and it was going to be a very different Chelsea that they faced in the second leg, because by then we were to have a new manager.

That Saturday we beat Barnsley 2-0 at home and that was to be Ruud's last game, though at the time there were no clues as to the bombshell about to hit. The following Thursday afternoon, after training, there was a buzz that something was happening – more gossip than anything. But there were no hints or clues from the Bridge and everything seemed pretty much as normal.

People have the idea that players know everything that is going on at a football club. Nothing could be further from the truth. That is evident in both the departure of Ruud Gullit and the boardroom power struggle between the late Matthew Harding and Ken Bates.

As for Ruud, there had been speculation about his future for some months. But the players are no wiser than the fans or the general public about what is going on. Everyone thought that he was going to sign a new contract and make sure there was continuity and stability at Stamford Bridge. But that Thursday afternoon the chief executive Colin Hutchinson showed up at the training ground to meet with Ruud. Then he left and we were told the news: Ruud was no longer in a job. There had been no indication that was going to happen. People outside the club assume we must have known but that just wasn't the case. What happens between the chairman and the manager happens in the boardroom or in the manager's office, not in the middle of the training pitch. We just do not know what is happening or being said. If a manager has been sacked or resigns, we are told before it is released to the press. Sometimes we know the day before.

But we are never told why. We are the employees of Chelsea Football Club and we are paid to play, not to be involved in the internal politics of the club. That was also the case with Matthew Harding and Ken Bates. I didn't come into too much contact with Matthew Harding. I knew he wanted to take over from Ken Bates at some stage but a lot of the talks and discussions were not for our ears and we were not party to what was being said. At one stage the fans were beginning to think that Matthew Harding was the right person for the job. But, as far as I'm concerned, Ken Bates started off the job of rebuilding Chelsea and I am sure he will finish it.

Matthew Harding came into the picture to help the situation at Chelsea but soon it was clear there had been an argument between the two of them, Bates and Harding. They were both strong personalities and, when two people like that disagree – and they clearly did – something had to give.

Players, however, do not get involved when that kind of debate is going on. It is not our place. On a personal level all I will say is that I've always liked Ken Bates. He has always been my favourite chairman. Not because he is my chairman now but because of the way he has handled me and looked after me. We seem to think alike. He appreciates what I have done for him and the club and I appreciate what he has done for me. Even if Matthew Harding had taken over, I would still have been a Ken Bates man because of what he has done for me and for Chelsea Football Club. Whether or not I would have got on with Matthew Harding, I will never know because of his tragic death. But the point I am making is that the players don't know the details of what is going on inside the boardroom. You are bound to hear rumours and whispers, but that is all you hear. We never know for sure until we are told like everyone else.

Going back to Ruud, the contract talks had started with him a good few months before he left. I could see why the club were trying to secure an arrangement with him because they wanted to avoid the situation they had found themselves in with Glenn Hoddle two seasons earlier. They didn't want to be stuck without a manager at the end of the season. They wanted something signed, sealed and delivered. But the talks didn't work out. Of course there were stories about Ruud's pay demands but to this day I do not know the full story of what went on in those discussions – and neither do I have a right to know. It was private, between Ruud and the club. All I knew was that Ruud had left the club.

Chapter 19

vialli, vialli . . .

For me, making Gianluca Vialli the manager of Chelsea was the best decision the club could have made . . . and I am not just saying that because he is still my boss. The players liked him and respected him and we were particularly impressed with the way he handled the situation with Ruud. He was clearly upset at the way he felt he was being treated but he did nothing to rock the boat or unsettle the squad. A great professional is Luca. He is a strong personality. On the outside he always seems very calm but believe me he has this burning desire to be successful. He is very ambitious. He has done so much in the game but he wants to do more. He also has this great presence and that was a major asset. Not many people could have followed a big person like Ruud. Luca, though, was one of them.

And what a first game for him . . . the second leg of the semi-final against Arsenal in the Coca-Cola Cup. It was clear very soon that we were going to play things differently under Luca. In training we were working straight away on a 4-3-3 system with a front trio of Mark Hughes, Franco Zola and Luca himself, rather than with Ruud's 4-4-2 formation. Luca is very tactically aware and made it very clear what he wanted to do and drew up the best way to play against Arsenal to cancel out their strengths. From our previous two matches against them that season, we were aware that they liked to play the ball from the back. That night Luca decided we were going to press them and give them no time on the ball at all.

It was a hell of a first game for Luca and he did look a bit edgy and nervous. It seemed to me he was finding it really difficult as a manager early on because it genuinely upset him to leave anybody out. Luca was edgy and it showed. We were all a lot closer to Luca than we were to Ruud and he felt bad about upsetting anyone. The dressing room before the game was a bit tense. It was a huge game and it was a big, big night for Luca. But then he produced a masterstroke to calm everyone's nerves.

In he walked with a bottle of champagne, gave everyone a glass and raised his. 'All the best to all of you,' he said. 'Good luck. All I can ask for is that you do your best. Help me if you can because I am going to need your help.' It was the most amazing pre-match scenario I had ever experienced. It was a lovely gesture, it put everyone at ease and we went on to win 3-1 to give Luca the perfect start. One match and he had taken us to Wembley . . . it couldn't have got any better. After going out of the FA Cup so early we were determined to make the most of the Coca-Cola Cup and get back to Wembley again if we could. We were so up for the game it was unbelievable. Arsenal had their full-strength side out, so did we, and on the night we produced the goods.

After the game came another glimpse of the difference in characters between Ruud and Luca. Myself, Dan Petrescu and Roberto di Matteo were sitting in the bath when he came in and said, 'I would like to thank you three for what you did tonight. You were magnificent. Thank you.' We all just looked at each other. It was the type of thing that Ruud would never have done but Luca has a totally different make-up.

Luca is so precise about everything, which used to drive me mad when we were rooming together when he was a player. Everything about him was perfect – his shirt was perfectly ironed, his shoes were shined to perfection. He carried this little suitcase about with him and he laid everything out on his bed – T-shirts, pants, socks, slippers. It was also neat and precise and sometimes I just wanted to go over there and mess it all up. I am not the tidiest person on the planet and it used to wind me up how everything was so ordered about Luca. I am not the person you want around if want order and peace in your life.

Unfortunately we lost our way in the league after that semi-final win. Maybe the prospect of the cup final was a distraction, I don't know. But we really struggled to find our form again – so much so that we lost six of our next seven games. The only win was against Crystal Palace and, although we were also making good progress in the European Cup Winners' Cup at the time, we should really have pushed harder in the league.

But at least we had the chance of more Wembley glory in the Coca-Cola Cup final – and it happened to be against the team we beat in the previous season's FA Cup final, Middlesbrough. This, though, was a different Middlesbrough. They were a stronger, more confident unit than the one we had faced ten months earlier. That team had been relegated and they had not proved the toughest opposition the previous year. Their confidence had gone and, once we took that lead inside 43 seconds, it was game over. We knew it.

This time it was different. Promotion was a certainty for them and, whereas they were a team used to losing when we met them before, this time they were a team used to winning. That was always going to make them more dangerous. They had also signed some proven quality players like Paul Merson and Andy Townsend as well as Gazza. But even so, we still fancied our chances of beating them.

The big decision for Luca was to choose between Frank Sinclair and Steve Clarke and again there was a remarkable insight into the difference between Luca and Ruud. As I've said, Ruud's way was to stick the team up on the wall 90 minutes before the game, no debate, no explanation, nothing. Luca was totally different – as me and Steve Clarke found out in our hotel room before the game. He came in and said, 'Clarkey, I need to have a word with you.' He was very nervous and almost shaking. He was very sad and clearly upset. 'I have to put you as a substitute,' he said. The look of disappointment on Clarkey's face had to be seen to be believed. 'Oh, f . . .ing hell, Luca,' Clarkey said.

Then Luca hit us with a real bombshell: 'Look, Clarkey, I am not even going to be sub because there are people ahead of me who deserve a medal.' He went to leave the room and Steve said, 'Luca, it's your decision and I respect that. But promise me one thing if you can – if we are winning 2-0 or 3-0, just let me play for 20 minutes.' 'I promise I will do that,' said Luca.

After he had gone, I turned to Steve and said, 'Do you realise what he's done? He hasn't even put himself on the bench. He could have but he's let one of the lads get the chance of a medal instead.' We agreed it was one hell of a gesture and between us hatched a plan as our way of saying thank you to him. If we won, we would insist he went up to get the cup. And that is what happened.

As we expected, the game was a lot tougher than the FA Cup final. Our fans were singing 'We're gonna score in a minute' just after the kick-off, referring to Roberto di Matteo's goal in the FA Cup final, but we knew it would be a lot harder this time. In fact, they took us into extra-time but Frank Sinclair and di Matteo again got the goals . . . and Steve got his 20 minutes.

After we celebrated at the final whistle I told Luca of the plan for him to get the cup. 'Go on,' I said, 'it's what the lads want.' He was so, so chuffed. He had played in so many of the matches to get us to the final and then left himself out. It was our personal tribute to him.

Once again, I took a kid out of the crowd, one decked in his Chelsea kit, and you will see him in all the photos. And just as at the cup final the year before I stayed on there as long as I could. I made a big mistake when we won the FA Cup with Wimbledon. Bobby Gould had said to stay out there as long as possible to enjoy everything about the wonderful moment. What happened? I couldn't wait to get into the dressing room to celebrate. These days, if ever I am involved in a final, it is the crowd who are home before me.

Chapter 20

the european cup winners' cup

During the 1997-98 season we were beginning to show the quality that all teams need if they are going to challenge for the championship: consistency. After all, consistency is the greatest test of any team. You need it. You need to feel that, when you step out on that field in a Chelsea shirt, you are not going to get beaten. And we had that air of supremacy – of invincibility if you like – in Europe.

We started the Cup Winners' Cup campaign against Slovan Bratislava. Although we had the disadvantage of playing the first leg at home (teams usually prefer to know exactly what they have to do in the second leg and prefer to play that game at home) it was really no big deal. We were so superior to them that I reckon we could have played both games at their place and still come out on top. We won 2-0 at home at a canter with goals from Roberto di Matteo and Danny Granville and by the same score away with Roberto and Luca Vialli getting one each. Really it could have been more.

The second-round tie in Norway against Tromso was nowhere near as easy, not in the first leg anyway. It was a match that by anybody's standards should not have been played. The snow was relentless and Ruud – who was in charge at the time – went spare trying to get the game called off. Passing the ball around was impossible and the conditions certainly suited Tromso and they made really good use of them.

They were a typical Scandinavian team . . . very big, strong and physical. They weren't too worried about the finer points of the game and at every dead ball situation they gave us huge problems. The man taking the kick would make a little mound of snow to give the ball more elevation. I went into the game suffering from a toe injury and I have to admit that the freezing weather did me one favour – my toe was numb after about five minutes and I just couldn't feel the pain. Ruud was doing all he could to get the game abandoned but the UEFA people insisted it went ahead. It was farce at times because they had to keep stopping play to paint the lines orange, so they could be seen through the snow. With just a minute left we were trailing 3-1 but Luca came to the rescue with a last-minute goal. Although we still lost we were not unhappy to come away from there with just one goal to find and two away goals under our belt.

Mind you, their players were confident enough. I went up to one of them afterwards to shake his hand and he said, 'Okay then, we will see you at your place.' 'I'll be there,' I said. 'Only I'd better tell you that we'll be playing on grass in London. You won't find it so easy.' 'Yes we will . . . ' he said, very cockily. ' . . . and we will beat you 3-0.'

Rule one in football: never wind up the opposition when you still have to play them away, and that bloke certainly wound me up.

Back at Stamford Bridge we won 7-1 and I couldn't wait to see that guy at the end. 'A bit different than snow, isn't it?' I said. 'We're a lot better on grass.' Tromso were full of themselves going into that game and we gave them a bloody good hiding. Nothing gave me greater pleasure.

In the quarter-final we were drawn against one of the favourites for the competition, Real Betis of Spain. Spanish teams are always hard. They are inevitably well organised at the back and have forwards with speed and skill. Again we were drawn away first and I have to admit that we would have settled for a draw. But it was better than that. Tore Andre Flo was on fire that night and scored twice in the first 15 minutes. To all intents and purposes, the tie was over. They pulled one back in the first minute of the second half but we held on reasonably comfortably to take a 2-1 lead back to Stamford Bridge. In the second leg, Betis took the lead but in truth we were never really in much danger and Frank Sinclair, Roberto di Matteo and Franco Zola scored to seal a 3-1 win and put us in the semi-final against Italian club Vicenza.

By then, of course, Luca was in charge and I sensed he was very nervous about the tie. Being Italian, he knew how they would be preparing to meet us. He knew they would have a game plan to frustrate us and he was very anxious about us being caught on the break. So in the away leg, we didn't play our normal positive game and we were content to sit back. Personally, I think that was something of a mistake because it gave them the initiative. We are not a good team when we do that. Consequently, they dominated the game and deserved to win with a goal from Zauli after 16 minutes. So we had no away goal to help us in the second leg and we were playing against a team who knew how to defend.

The omens were not good but the second leg at Stamford Bridge turned out to be one of the most eventful and exciting matches in which I have been involved. With one goal to pull back, teams tend to be a bit wary. Their approach to the game can be awkward. They are reluctant to go flat out from the start because such a commitment leaves them open to the counter-attack. And Italians counter-attack for fun. As far as we were concerned, on the one hand we wanted to be patient but on the other we wanted to make use of the home advantage. Somehow we had to strike a balance. After half-an-hour, though, the decision on how we should play the game was made for us when their striker Luiso put them ahead. Suddenly we were in all sorts of trouble.

After he scored, Luiso ran round in front of our fans with his finger over his lips to imply that he had shut them up. That got right up my nose. It got to the rest of the lads as well and all we really wanted to do was give him a boot up the backside. He shouldn't have been doing that to our crowd at our ground. It was really taking the mickey. What we desperately needed, though, was a goal, and quickly, because by then we needed three to win the tie.

Gus Poyet got us that first one and at half-time we were all very

positive. Whatever else you might say about this team, we had belief –
and we believed we could reach the final. Five minutes into the second
half Franco got a second goal to put us ahead on the night. We were still
behind because of the away goal but we had the best part of 40 minutes
to get the third goal that would put us through. Our saviour turned out
to be Mark Hughes. He is the strong, brave type of striker that
continental defenders hate to face and he made an impact five minutes
after coming on as a 70th-minute substitute. As the ball came in he won
an aerial challenge, flicked the ball over the defender's head and scored
with a stunning volley. It was the kind of goal that you dream about
scoring. Along with the rest of Stamford Bridge, I went mad.

Then Vicenza knew they had to come out and try to get a second
goal. It was real ding-dong stuff, the ball was zipping from one end of
the field to the other. The passion in the crowd became so intense that
both teams got caught with it.

In the last minute – literally the last kick of the game – Ed De Goey
became another hero of the night. Vicenza broke away and the ball fell
to our mate Luiso. He looked a certainty to score until Ed somehow
scooped the ball off his foot and away for a corner. They took it, the ref
blew and I made a beeline for Ed to give him one huge hug. I just went
potty. Then I went to Luiso to let him know what I felt about his
gesture to our fans after he scored – and I gave their supporters the
same 'sshhhh' treatment as I went off.

It was one hell of a night and one hell of a game. It hadn't been like
a typical cat-and-mouse European match. They are usually cagey
matches but this one had the lot . . . pace, passion and an excellent
referee who let the game flow. Now we were ready for our second final
of the season, against Stuttgart in Stockholm.

Stockholm? They might as well have played the game at Stamford
Bridge. The whole stadium seemed to be decked out in blue and white.
When they are outnumbered, our fans can usually be heard. When
they outnumber the other supporters by five to one, then it's just like a
home game.

We felt so good going into that game. Things were starting to go right – like getting Gus Poyet back to fitness after his long lay-off. He is a hell of a player is Gus and he showed his value in the semi-final when equalising within a couple of minutes of us falling two goals behind on aggregate. I felt great that night, we had so much experience in that team with players like Roberto di Matteo, Gus, Luca and our tremendous goalkeeper, Ed de Goey. I knew they had seen all this kind of thing before and knew exactly how to handle the occasion. That was a great help and gave us an extra edge. I just knew we were going to win

We knew for certain that Stuttgart would be a strong and disciplined side. There was all sorts of talk of the injury problems they had going into the final but we paid no attention to that. We knew they would be difficult to break down and that they would have virtually their strongest team out that night. I never thought for one minute that it would be a classic match. We expected the Germans to soak up the pressure and then try to hit us on the break. They are brilliant at that ploy and we were not disappointed by their approach. The game was predictably close and it took another inspired substitution to open up Stuttgart.

Once again, it came in the 70th minute but, while Mark Hughes was the hero in the semi-final, this time it was Franco Zola who came good for us. He came on for Tore Andre Flo and immediately adjusted to the pace and tempo of the game. He made a darting run into the Stuttgart penalty area, I spotted the space he had made for himself and just played the ball through. Franco took one touch and produced a fantastic finish. It was world-class to produce that kind of skill and show that kind of composure after being on the field for such a short while. It was a wonderful goal that capped a wonderful night for our fans and the team. Stuttgart just didn't have anything left to come back at us.

Come the final whistle we staged our pre-rehearsed celebration. We all linked hands and made a sprint to the middle of the pitch before producing a mass dive. Then we stood up and, still holding hands, we went down on our knees, raised our arms and bowed in a gesture of worship to our fans. It was our way of saying thank you to them. They had spent an awful lot of money and used up holidays and all sorts to follow us all over Europe during the competition and we valued their support.

The celebration on the pitch was excellent and the dressing room afterwards was one noisy place with just about every language in Europe being heard. Once again, I milked the moment. It meant as much to me as anyone. All those barren years I had spent at Chelsea waiting for things to take off and the last three seasons had made it all worthwhile. I thought long and hard about it all on that trip home. I had to pinch myself to make sure all this was happening to me.

But, if I have one regret about that night, it is that we had no great public celebration. I would have loved to parade the two cups we won – the Coca-Cola Cup and the Cup Winners' Cup – around Chelsea in an open-top bus. But we had a commitment as a club to go on tour the following day and so we went straight from Sweden to Heathrow, had a couple of hours' wait and then left for the Far East. It was a shame because I would have loved to show our tremendous supporters what we had won.

Chapter 21

19 games unbeaten

The 1998-99 season had all the makings of a memorable one, although for me it was to be for the wrong reasons. I seemed to be the best paid spectator at Stamford Bridge for much of it. The pre-season had gone well and Luca Vialli had not wasted any time in trying to build on the success of the previous season. He followed the old football adage that the time to build is when you are at your strongest. Four new players had come to the club: Pierluigi Casiraghi, Albert Ferrer, Brian Laudrup and Marcel Desailly.

With Marcel joining Frank Leboeuf, it meant we had two World Cup winners in the squad from the French team that beat Brazil – and Frank wasn't slow in reminding us what he had achieved when he came back for pre-season. He was excited, and rightly so. If I had a World Cup winner's medal, I would be full of it as well.

Good luck to him as far as I'm concerned. He had won football's greatest honour. They tried taking the mickey out of him on that television show *They Think It's All Over* but it didn't worry him one bit because he had the medal and no one could take it away from him. To be fair to him, he has always acknowledged what he owes to Chelsea. Before he joined us, no one had really heard of him but he has grown in stature since coming to Stamford Bridge. He is one of the best sweeping central defenders this club has ever had. He has been great for us and I am just pleased we signed him.

Actually, Ruud Gullit, who signed Frank, had Laurent Blanc down as his first choice and so it was ironic that Frank owed his place in the

World Cup final to Blanc's suspension for being sent off against Croatia. In fact, when I heard that Blanc was going to be out of the final, I rang Frank and left a message on his mobile. It was on the lines of, 'You lucky French so-and-so'. When France won we all knew exactly what would happen when he came back to the club. The first order was to make the doors around the place bigger because there was no way he was going to be able to fit through them.

Marcel is a totally different character from Frank. He has a terrific sense of humour but is very laid back. That's off the field. On it, he is so powerful. He is one of the most natural athletes I have ever seen. As well as his strength in the tackle, he is a tremendous ball player. He has got everything you want in a modern player, the lot. You get the feeling he could play anywhere on the field and be comfortable. He is also a real man-mountain which is handy for me on the pitch . . . I can hide behind him and throw punches.

We reported back on a real high and, after seeing what new players had been brought in, there was a genuine feeling that we could now go and win more. We had bought four quality men, although we had lost Mark Hughes to Southampton. Casi seemed an ideal replacement for Hughesie, Brian Laudrup came down from Glasgow Rangers to give us more options up front and Albert Ferrer proved to be a really consistent and very able defender. We had cover and we had strength in depth.

There were real grounds for optimism. The signings of Marcel and Casi were tremendous. Both should have been worth more than £10 million each, yet we got the pair of them for that figure. That was good business by the club. And they were among the best available in their respective positions. No wonder there was a feeling we could now go one step on from our success in the cups and take that league title. That was the next major trophy that we had in our sights.

As well as world-class players in the squad the club and the ground were being completely transformed. When I signed, there was a poxy little club office in a building which had ivy climbing up the walls. Now Stamford Bridge is one of the best stadiums in the country, complete with a hotel, restaurants and bars. It oozes class and that speaks volumes for what the chairman has done for the place.

The players who had been involved in the World Cup came back a week later than the rest of us and joined up with the squad at our pre-season base in Holland. Luca was determined that we should be spot-on for the long season ahead and had arranged some special games for us against local sides when we would play ten against their full elevens. It was hard work but it was worthwhile. The confidence was growing and the goals were going in.

Casi was showing what a great asset he was going to be. After losing Mark Hughes, I thought that one area where we could be lacking was a target man up front. But Casi was proving to be different class in that department. He was not afraid of the physical side of the game and put himself about more than enough. He also had great touch. Like Hughesie, he had never been a prolific goalscorer but he got his share and was superb at setting up goals for other people. He was comfortable with his back to the goal and was not afraid of getting hurt. When he was to get a serious injury quite early in the season, it was to prove a big, big blow to us. But in Holland it all seemed to be going so well, until I had the first experience of what was to be the worst disciplinary season of my career.

We were playing in a pre-season tournament match against Atletico Madrid and I was involved in a tussle with one of their players. We were both sent off. We were then suspended for the next game in the tournament and I thought that would be the end of it.

The Spanish FA looked at the case and decided that was the end of it; they wouldn't take it any further. Our FA? When they got the report, they handed me a three-match ban which was to come into force during the second week of the season. What really annoyed me was that there was a total lack of consistency. Paul Merson got sent off in a pre-season game and yet that red card was quashed, and another player, a Brazilian, was sent off in the tournament in Holland and his FA did nothing. Yet I was banned.

From feeling on top of the world when I went out to Holland I came back feeling totally demoralised. I was to miss the games against Newcastle, Arsenal and Nottingham Forest. And, when I did start playing in the Premiership again, I was injured against Blackburn and had to come off. It was like some terrible omen for me.

If the FA weren't in the mood to do me any favours, they were no kinder to Chelsea Football Club. Because Cup Winners' Cup matches were played on a Thursday night and often involved returning to England in the early hours of Friday morning, there was an agreement that after each European match we would be given a home league game on the Sunday. What happened? Because of what we were told was a fault with the computer we were in fact given an away game. And not just round the corner, either. During the course of the season we had to go to places like Liverpool, Leeds and Sheffield after our European trips. That did us no favours at all. I would have thought they could have changed it quite easily by turning those away games into home games. No, they said, it couldn't be done. Why, I don't know.

They could, however, do Chelsea one favour in the future . . . not give us Coventry away in the first game of the season. Without a doubt, Coventry are our bogey side. We always seem to play well at Highfield Road and always seem to end up on the wrong end of the scoreline. It was no different that season. After looking a bit sleepy for the first 20 minutes, we dominated the game. The problem was we went two goals down in that opening period and, although Gus Poyet pulled a goal back for us, we just couldn't get the equaliser that we deserved on the run of play. But you have to keep in mind that we were still learning as a team, still trying to gel, and we started to put things right straight away.

In fact, we weren't to be beaten again until December when we went out of the Worthington Cup to Wimbledon. That was one hell of a run by anyone's standards. The strategy that Luca had drawn up was a simple one but one we felt we could achieve: we draw the away games and win the home ones. That, he reckoned, should keep us in touch with the top of the table. We recovered from that bad start to draw at home with Newcastle and, despite the result, we knew we were getting that bit better all the time.

That showed in our next game – the European Super Cup played between the Champions League winners and the Cup Winners' Cup winners. We were up against Real Madrid in Monaco. A lot of people knocked the game, saying it meant nothing. But I can tell you that it meant a lot to the Chelsea players and, judging by the way Real Madrid played, it also meant a lot to them, you could see how disappointed the Madrid players were at the end. Gus Poyet won it for us with a goal in the second half. For me, it was just one more example of how my career had progressed. After all those years without winning a thing, there I was picking up my fourth major trophy in less than two years. That meant a lot to me.

Back in league action, we drew 0-0 at home to Arsenal. Lee Dixon was sent off in what was a good competitive match. It was the second match of my ban, so I had to watch and I thought we were going to get all three points from the penalty spot when Casi was fouled. But nothing was given and we had to settle for a point.

I was still having to watch when we secured our first league win of the season, against Nottingham Forest at home, but I was back when we played our first European Cup Winners' Cup match against Helsingborgs at Stamford Bridge. They made life very difficult for us but we still managed to create quite a few chances. However, we took only one of them, when Frank Leboeuf scored. We were happy enough at 1-0, though. We were learning all the time in Europe and the most important lesson of all is not to concede a goal to the away team. More often than not, 0-0 is a decent result because the onus is then on the other team to come at you at their place and in doing so they can leave gaps. At Chelsea we have players not only with talent but also with the know-how to make the most of that kind of situation.

A big match for us came next in the league: away to Blackburn. We badly wanted to do well up there because we never seemed to do ourselves justice at Ewood Park. That night we did. We won 4-3 in what was my first league game since my ban. But it was victory at a price. I was injured and had to go off and Graeme Le Saux, a former Blackburn player, was sent off after a tussle on the touchline with one of their players. It was also the night that Tore Andre Flo came up trumps again when he came on as substitute along with Brian Laudrup. They turned the game around for us.

It was around that time that there were the first whispers that Brian Laudrup wasn't settled at the club and wanted to go back to Denmark. I had found Brian something of a loner since he came to the club. He preferred his own company, it was as simple as that. I roomed with him when he came over to Holland pre-season and he was the kind of bloke who just wanted his own space. He wasn't rude or anything but he just didn't speak a lot, he preferred to be quiet and left alone.

It came as a shock to many people when he said he wanted to leave and return home to Denmark. He took a lot of stick for it but in my mind he showed a lot of balls. He was forever being asked about all the money he was earning and there was one occasion in Monaco when, at a press conference, he was quizzed about how he could justify earning so much money. I was with him and just said to the journalist,'So if you are offered £50,000 a week to go and work somewhere else, you wouldn't take it? Of course you would.' Many people thought that Brian was just here for the cash but, as I saw it, there wasn't a problem with what he was earning. Chelsea Football Club wanted to pay him the money and I can't see how that can be anyone's business but his and the club's. As long as both sides agree, where's the problem and why should people harp on about it?

I felt sorry for Brian. In fact, if you think about it, what he did was the right thing. He could easily have stayed at Chelsea, picked up his wages and just not tried. You can't make a player do well. You can't force him to enjoy his football. If money was his motivation, he could have stayed, taken it and just not bothered. But he was honest enough to say he wasn't happy, his family wasn't happy and that, after spending so many years playing abroad, he wanted to go home. I can tell you, as far as I am concerned, everyone at the club had the utmost respect for him and what he did. He took a cut in wages to go back to

Denmark, so how was he in football just for the cash?

Laudrup was in fact a true professional, as he proved in his last game for Chelsea. It was a cup-tie against the club he was going to join – and he scored the goal that knocked them out. You can't be more professional than that. For me, he is to be admired and respected for that, not slaughtered.

I missed the next three matches because of the injury I picked up at Blackburn: the home game with Middlesborough that we won 2-0, the away leg against Helsingborgs that we drew 0-0 and the 1-1 draw against Liverpool at Anfield. I made my comeback as a substitute in the 2-1 home win against Charlton. They made it hard for us and, although we managed to beat them, it was tough going. It was a game we needed to win to keep the momentum of our season going. We still had to reach our best as the new players settled in but, while they were doing that, we were staying among the front-runners and that was important.

In the second round of the Cup Winners' Cup we were drawn against the team Brian Laudrup was going to join, FC Copenhagen. It was not the best of performances at home where we drew 1-1. In fact they took the lead following a mix-up between Marcel Desailly and myself. The man to benefit was Bjarne Goldbaek – later to join us – who hit a ferocious shot into the net. But late on Marcel hit an equaliser and we were happy enough with a draw in the end against a well-organised side who had come to Stamford Bridge to sit back and hit us on the break.

The following Sunday we were at Elland Road and thought we had a good chance of winning. But Frank Leboeuf was sent off for getting two yellow cards and in the end we grateful for a point after Jimmy Floyd Hasselbaink forced Ed de Goey into making two great saves.

Then came disciplinary problem number two for me against Aston Villa in the Worthington Cup. We were winning the game comfortably 4-1 and there were just a couple of minutes to go when, quite simply, I had a brainstorm. I launched myself into a tackle and, although I honestly didn't set out to hurt their player, I accept that it must have looked awful. I didn't actually touch him but the reaction of all the Aston Villa players didn't help me at all. They all came running over screaming and shouting and I have to be grateful to Michael Duberry, who blocked Alan Thompson as he was coming to take issue with me. It was another instance of my competitive streak getting me into trouble and I was just plain stupid. There was no excuse. All I can say is that, if there is a tackle to be won, if it is the first minute or the 90th, if we are 4-1 up or 4-1 down, I will try to get the ball. That is just my way.

After Villa in the cup we were due to play Villa in the Premiership, which they were leading at that time. But the game was rained off, which meant that our next game was Brian Laudrup's last. And, after losing one quality player who had joined us in the summer on the Thursday, we lost another one three days later at West Ham when Casi picked up a terrible injury. He went down in our 1-1 draw against West Ham at Upton Park after he collided with their goalkeeper Shaka Hislop. He fell really badly and was clearly in an awful lot of pain. It really had to be bad for Casi to just lie there. Since he arrived at the club he showed himself to be very brave physically and to be able to take the knocks as well as anyone and better than most. After all, he had been brought up in Italian football where strikers have it really hard. He had scars on his legs and around his eyes.

As Casi lay there a number of the team were not at all happy with the way the ambulance people went about helping him. Mike Banks, our physiotherapist, kept asking for a certain piece of equipment to be brought on. 'What is it, what is it?' was all they kept saying. They kept bringing this stretcher out but Mike kept saying that was not what he wanted. He wanted a special thing that you put round a leg when it is badly injured. Eventually, after they brought the stretcher on once again, I just reacted and kicked it off. The referee Graham Barber said to me, 'Calm down, calm down.' I think he was frightened I might boot someone. Calm down? I was fuming. I wanted Casi to have the right treatment for what was clearly a serious injury. Eventually Casi was taken off and we went on to get a draw.

Everyone had felt a bit flat going into that game because of our trip to Copenhagen the week before and, now that we'd lost Casi, we all felt even worse. His loss was a huge blow to the team. We had no one else like him at the club and he was emerging as the perfect man to lead the line. And we weren't able to fill the gap he left. Not properly, anyway.

A few days later we signed the man who had nearly put us out of the Cup Winners' Cup, Bjarne Goldbaek. He had looked a good, busy player against us in the two games and we signed him for a bargain £300,000. When he arrived, I demanded some of his wages or part of his signing-on fee. 'It's because of me – and my mistake – that you're here,' I told him. 'I set you up for your goal and because of that you are now a Chelsea player. I got you your move to England.' He loved all that kind of banter.

Anyway, after the West Ham game we had an incredible Worthington Cup match against Arsenal at Highbury. I missed it because by then my suspension had come through from the red card against Villa in the previous round. We won the game 5-0 but no one was getting really carried away because, although we won really well and played some great stuff, Arsenal had a lot of reserves in their line-up that night. But you can only beat what is put out in front of you and we did that convincingly enough.

I missed the home league games with Wimbledon and Sheffield Wednesday and the away one against Leicester. We could have won all three but drew at home to Wednesday. We were up there in fourth place, nicely placed just behind the top teams, and I always felt we could get that much better as the season went on. With the ban now finished, I was available again for our next game in the Worthington Cup at Wimbledon. We really should not have lost that night because we had so much of the play but that Dons fighting spirit saw them through against us, 2-1. There was some talk that the Worthington Cup was the least of our priorities but there was no talking like that at Chelsea. When we go in for a competition, we want to win it, don't worry about that, and we were upset at going out to Wimbledon.

Although it wasn't a big deal, we were also disappointed to lose

our unbeaten run. Nineteen games without defeat equalled the club
record. However, Chelsea are a top team and we had to learn to put
setbacks behind us and get back to the business of winning.

Chapter 22

ups and downs

The next game after Wimbledon was at Everton in the league. Before it I made one of the biggest mistakes of my life. You would have thought by now I would have learned but I let my guard down in a press conference before the game. 'I will not get sent off again,' I said when I was asked about how I would handle myself in the future. After 35 minutes at Goodison Park I was back in the dressing room after being shown two yellow cards.

In my defence, I reckon it was a joke. If I am in the wrong, as I was with my tackle against Aston Villa in the Worthington Cup, then I will be the first to admit it. This time, it just wasn't warranted. The referee was Gary Willard and he booked me for my first tackle of the game. Their striker, Danny Cadamarteri, was a bit too quick for me as he nicked the ball away. I stopped the challenge but slid along the ground. I couldn't do anything about it. I never actually caught him but he had to jump over me and, as he landed, he tumbled over. I picked him up, asked him if he was alright, he said yes and there was no problem.

But Willard booked me. 'That's the first thing I've done,' I said. But he is one of those referees you can't talk to. He seems to want to be the centre of attention and wants everyone to know he is the referee and that he is in charge. I like referees who stay in the background and let the players get on with it. It seems to me there are referees who want to be the star of the show instead of keeping out of the way and doing their job like they should do.

Worse was to come for me in the 34th minute. I was running towards the Everton goal and their Italian defender Marco Materazzi toed the ball away and I just left my foot dangling. It wasn't malicious or anything like that. I accidentally caught him and he fell over. He got up and I asked him if he was okay and he said yes. But the crowd were whistling and, when the ball went out of play about two minutes later, Gary Willard came running over to me and showed me a second yellow. I was dumbstruck. I just said, 'Watch the video, watch the f . . . ing video.' He just said, 'Off,' so I had no option but to go.

I was sick about it, especially when I later saw him referee a match between Manchester United and Arsenal. I saw Patrick Vieira and Roy Keane kick each other and then push and shove each other. What did Gary Willard do? Nothing. He just had a word with them. I was amazed. Why, I thought, didn't he do the same with them as he did with me? There should be no middle, no in-between. It was so blatant what had gone on between Vieira and Keane, everyone had seen it. And yet when I played up at Old Trafford for Chelsea, myself and David Beckham were going for a ball from Franco Zola and I shoulder-charged him, nothing more than that. He fell over, the crowd whistled and then Willard came over and booked me. I watched it later on the video and he hadn't seen the incident. Yet he booked me. Vieira and Keane scrap in front of his eyes and he does nothing.

After Willard cautioned me for the Beckham clash, I remember saying to him, 'You didn't see anything,' and I then pointed to my ears and said, 'You are listening to them.' There is no doubt in my mind that some referees are influenced by the home crowd. Two exceptions are Mike Reed and Graham Poll. They treat players like men. They do their job and, if you have a go at them, they will have a go back. Gary Willard is one to whom you just cannot say a word, he doesn't want to know.

Normally it is just a one-match ban for a dismissal for two yellows but, because I had been sent off twice before in the season, I got two extra matches under the new system. And I can't see how that is right either. If you are sent off, you get punished and, as far as I am concerned, that should be the end of it. But under the system they have now, you are being punished twice. That cannot be right. I am not telling the FA how to do their job but I cannot for the life of me see the justification in punishing someone again when they are already facing disciplinary action.

I was made substitute for our next game which was the rearranged match at home to Aston Villa. We won that 2-1 with a last-minute goal from Tore Andre Flo. Then came two tough away games at Derby and Manchester United. At Derby, though, we should have won. We were the better side and we were leading 2-1 with about a minute to go when there was a mix-up between Graeme Le Saux and Ed de Goey. The ball broke to Dean Sturridge and we had lost two points – two points which would have taken us to the top of the Premiership. It was definitely a chance missed.

Next we had to go to Old Trafford and, although 1-1 was a decent result that most teams would settle for up there, we were disappointed that we didn't win. Alex Ferguson said afterwards that we were the best team they had played and I have to admit we did do well that night.

Three days later we did go to the top of the table after beating Tottenham 2-0 at home. George Graham had taken over at Tottenham and they were a very organised outfit, as you would expect. They were giving us problems when their striker Chris Armstrong was sent off for a second booking. The Tottenham players weren't happy with that decision – and neither were they happy with Frank Leboeuf, who ran a long way to make his feelings known to the referee. There was a lot of finger-pointing out on the field and all I could do was watch because the three-match ban from the dismissal at Everton had now come into force.

I had to watch the next two as well – at Southampton (won 2-0) and at home to Manchester United (drew 0-0) – before I was back for the start of our FA Cup run at Oldham. We won that comfortably enough, 2-0 but again we had problems with injuries. This time Tore Andre Flo hurt his ankle and we were now struggling for front players following the long-term loss of Casi and the decision of Brian Laudrup to go back to Denmark. Luca was under pressure to buy but he decided against it. He felt we were strong enough in that department and to be fair the results kept going our way.

We went to Newcastle and, quite naturally, a lot was made of Chelsea facing Ruud Gullit's new team. I never had the chance to speak to Ruud for any length of time that day but I did see him out on the pitch and shook his hand. Many people expected him to be bitter and twisted about what had happened to him at Chelsea, but not me. I know Ruud and I know he is not that kind of person.

Then it was Coventry at home and a fracas on the touchline which didn't involve me for a change. Coventry played well, they were really organised and were making it hard for us. Maybe a bit of frustration was coming into our game but at 1-1 the ball went out of play and their manager Gordon Strachan kept hold of it. Our masseur Terry Byrne tried to get the ball, so we could get the game going again, but the Coventry bench wouldn't let it go. There was a lot of verbals and fist-shaking but nothing really happened. In the tunnel afterwards there was some shoving and pushing but nothing too much really. You would be amazed at how many little flare-ups there are in the tunnels. But it is all soon forgotten.

We had the fright of our lives against Oxford in the FA Cup at their Manor Ground. Quite simply, we got away with murder that night and only stayed in the FA Cup because of a penalty that shouldn't have been given. Mike Reed gave it and he came in for a lot of criticism for the award. It was a lifeline to us. We were losing 1-0 and they were playing well above themselves. Then in the last minute their player Kevin Francis made a tackle on Luca inside the area. The slow-motion replay on video showed it wasn't a penalty but from where I was in the area there was the sound of boot on boot as Francis went in on Luca. Mike Reed heard the noise and gave us the spot-kick because he assumed Francis hadn't played the ball. He had but referees haven't got the benefit of slow-motion replays. Anyway, Frank Leboeuf put the kick away and we were still in the FA Cup . . . just. It was quite an eventful night all round for Frank. He was on the receiving end of a bad two-footed tackle in the second half and had to go off for treatment.

The Oxford manager Malcolm Shotton wasn't too impressed with Frank and let him know on the touchline. Apparently he suggested the debate be continued in the tunnel afterwards. I used to play against Shotton years ago and he seems like a very tough character. Anyway, I was delighted Frank scored from the spot because it was his way of putting two fingers up to him. Also, a replay wasn't the worst outcome for Oxford. They had been struggling for cash and they would get their cut from the receipts at Stamford Bridge.

At the end of January came our first league defeat since the opening day of the season, when we went to Highbury to play Arsenal. We played well that night, especially in the second half, but we lost to a goal we felt should not have been allowed. As the ball came over, Dan Petrescu was convinced he was fouled by Marc Overmars before he set up Dennis Bergkamp for the winner. Mind you, we were caught napping by the ball through and paid the price for that. We had lots of possession but just couldn't produce the finish to go with it.

Next came the Oxford replay – and another red card for me. I made two reflex handballs at either end of the pitch and Mike Reed sent me off. They were more instinctive than anything but under the rules about handball there was nothing I could do – except get ready for another spell of spectating. At least we ran out winners, 4-2 in the end, and I scored one of the goals.

Next we beat Southampton at home in the league in what was a really poor match and then recorded a good 1-0 win at Sheffield Wednesday in the FA Cup. Our next opponents were Blackburn and the match finished in a 1-1 draw. We finished with ten men because Luca was sent off – and afterwards Blackburn's Chris Sutton really sounded off about Frank Leboeuf. They had been at it throughout the game and there are always verbals in those situations. You accept it as part of the game and you don't go on about it afterwards like Sutton did. Anyway, I shouldn't think Frank was worried about it in the least.

A pretty comfortable 3-1 win at Forest kept us in second place and then came a controversial game against Liverpool at Stamford Bridge. The trouble was started when Michael Owen fouled Frank Leboeuf and the feuding carried on, notably between Robbie Fowler and Graeme Le Saux. I have since spoken to Graeme about what happened and he didn't have a problem with me telling what happened.

It wasn't the fact that Fowler showed him his backside that caused the problem. It was what Fowler said about Graeme and his family. There are some things that are off-limits and insulting someone else's family is one of them. It wasn't the rent boy thing. Players like Graeme and myself have had to put up with that for years. Opposition fans like calling us the 'Chelsea Rent Boys'. We just laugh. What Fowler said was different. It was out of order. And what wound Graeme up more was that Fowler was delaying him taking a free-kick and the linesman saw what was happening. But, instead of asking the linesman, the referee came straight over and booked Graeme for time wasting. That only made it worse. But we won, so that was perhaps the best answer we could give. Then we booked our place in the European Cup Winners' Cup semi-final with a 3-0 win in the first leg of the quarter-final against Valerenga of Norway at Stamford Bridge.

The FA Cup came next, another tie against Manchester United at Old Trafford. It ended up 0-0 but we both had a player sent off in what was never a dirty game. Roberto di Matteo went off for us and Paul Scholes went later. Because of the European commitments of both clubs, it was agreed that the usual ten-day rule between a cup match and a replay would be waived and three days later we met them again at Stamford Bridge. I played and I should have scored; United can thank Tore Andre Flo that I didn't. It was 1-0 to United at the time when Tore went up with Peter Schmeichel for a cross. The ball broke to me and I stabbed it towards the goal. It was going in, there was no question of that, but I was horrified to see Tore falling over and I could see what was going to happen. He tried desperately to get out of the way but the ball hit his leg and that took it wide. I could have cried. When things like that happen you know it's not going to be your night.

That was us out of the FA Cup as United got another to win 2-0.

We got another really bad result in the league when we lost 1-0 at home to West Ham. All they wanted to do was sit back and let us come on to them. They just soaked it up. Fair enough – it was up to us to break them down. More and more teams are playing like that when they come to Stamford Bridge and we regard it is a compliment to the quality of the team we have assembled. We had a few chances and Frank Leboeuf hit a shot really straight and powerful but Rio Ferdinand blocked it with his legs. West Ham's chances were few and far between but they produced a goal from a free-kick and Paul Kitson forced the ball home.

We were devastated, nothing seemed to be going our way. But one thing I am sure of: this Chelsea team has character. We came straight back with three wins – against Valerenga in the second leg, at Aston Villa in the Premiership and then at Charlton.

The first leg of the Cup Winners' Cup semi-final at home against Real Mallorca didn't go exactly to plan, though. We drew 1-1 and that was not a good result. As if that wasn't enough, I had to put up with ten days of worry to see if I would be able to play in the second leg. Television and then the papers made a big thing out of me appearing to bite their defender Marcelino. I never did; I just gestured to bite him after he had run his fingernails up my neck. He didn't complain, the referee saw nothing and Real Mallorca said nothing. But the next thing I knew UEFA were studying video evidence and I had been charged with misconduct. It was staggering. I made a statement about what happened and faxed it to them. They decided to take no further action.

We won at Wimbledon to keep the title hopes alive but then came a week when it really all seemed to go away from us. We went to Middlesbrough and we knew that, if we won, we would go top of the table at a crucial time of the season. But we drew 0-0 and we should have won because we had the best chance of a very tight game and it fell to the man you would want in a one-on-one situation with the goalkeeper: Franco Zola. But he hurried his shot, Mark Schwarzer saved and little Franco was bitterly upset afterwards. I tried to console him because he was so down. 'Look, Franco, there is no problem. We are not fussed. What happened just happened. No one is blaming you. What about the games you have won for us with your free-kicks? We are all in this together.'

But the real blow came in our next home game against Leicester. This was one we had to win, no question. And we looked as though we would be doing just that as we were two goals in front with less than ten minutes left. But then Michael Duberry scored an own-goal, and Steve Guppy scored an unbelievable equaliser for them, and it was 2-2. It had been little short of a disastrous ten days and to round it off, we lost 1-0 in the second leg in Mallorca.

The Mallorca fans made me a particular target after my 'biting' run-in with Marcelino in the first leg. When we went out training the day before the game, there were hundreds of kids watching and they kept barking at me like dogs. And the hostility continued in the match. They were at me from the time I went out for the warm-up.

We had a great celebration planned if I scored, and in the last minute I thought I was going to do just that when I went to meet Franco Zola's cross. But I headed it too deliberately and wide. Shame – because, if it had gone in, I was going to run to the corner in front of the Mallorca fans, go down on all fours like a dog, lift one leg and pretend to pee on the corner flag! But we weren't at our best that night and I think the Leicester result had taken a lot out of us mentally. After Mallorca we went to Sheffield Wednesday and drew 0-0 in a pretty average game. I couldn't help thinking that, when you look back at the really stupid points we dropped through the season, we could have had 70 points by the end of April and been well in front in the league.

If I had one wish for the season, it would have been that Luca had involved himself more. In my opinion, he didn't play himself enough. Luca is a proven striker and has great ability. And he also has the precious commodity of experience. There were several occasions when we could have used him to great effect, especially after the loss of Casi and Tore Andre Flo through injury. One occasion that really stands out is the second leg of the semi-final against Mallorca in Palma. It was a trophy we were desperate to win because it was the last Cup Winners' Cup ever and we wanted to be the first team to win it in consecutive seasons and be the last name on the list of winners.

We started at 1-1 and knew we had to score in front of one of the most hostile crowds I have come across in my career. Yes, I include Anfield and Old Trafford in that. It was a tight ground and a tense and passionate atmosphere – but for some reason, Luca didn't even put himself on the bench.

We could have done with him out there, particularly as the match wore on and we were trailing 1-0 on the night. We always had to score one goal but there was no Luca to come on. Knowing him as I do, he probably acted in the interests of the rest of the team. He hates hurting people, does Luca, but we needed him out there that night. We needed him to have been a bit more selfish when it came to team selection. A player like Luca coming on would frighten the life out of the opposition, particularly if there are something like 20 minutes to go and they think they have done the hard bit. He is someone who is highly likely to get a goal, as he has proved time and time again. Luca seems to have this golden rule: if he doesn't start the match, then he won't involve himself. Maybe he should be a bit more flexible in that thinking.

In the end 1998-99 proved to be a disappointing season for us. But it has also become apparent to me that the future of Chelsea is secure. I just look at young players like Jody Morris and Mikael Forssell. Jody has come on tremendously. He has matured and become more aware. On more than one occasion we played together in central midfield and you wouldn't have thought that was possible before. We seemed too similar but Jody is now able to broaden his game and has shown himself to be very talented. Mikael has incredible maturity for someone who is only just 18. He is strong and has shown a great eye for goal. All he needs to do now is work on the simple things like holding the ball up instead of trying to do a trick every time he gets it.

It is a strange feeling, as I write this now. For me – speaking as someone who has seen this club develop so dramatically in the last decade – Chelsea have reached another level and the team is now stronger than at any time. We have greater all-round strength and I can only see us improving. That, however, only makes it all the more frustrating that we haven't won one of the major trophies. But I still maintain that we have progressed. We have qualified to contest a place in the Champions League and that is a massive achievement for the club. We are used to being successful and that is an important mentality to have if you are going to be consistently successful. We are now looking, over the next four or five years, to be in that top three in the Premiership and, hopefully, to win the title as well. That is the next target in my sights. That is the aim of all really good teams, who don't just settle for the top six.

It is impossible to talk about the 1998-99 season without talking about Graham Rix. He is our first team coach who was sent to prison in March 1999 after he pleaded guilty to a charge of having unlawful sex with a 15-year-old girl. Graham was devastated and, despite how it looks and what the facts say, I can assure you all is not how it seemed. Graham is not an evil man; he just made a mistake. A stupid mistake.

I think I can best explain my view on the situation by referring to a letter that was sent to me by an irate season-ticket holder who was upset at the stance taken by the club over the whole business. The chairman Ken Bates and the chief executive Colin Hutchinson made it clear that, when Graham came out of prison, his job would be there waiting for him. This season-ticket holder took issue with that. He called that standpoint a disgrace and wrote to both myself as captain of the team and to Ken Bates as chairman. He said he had a 15-year-old daughter and found it abhorrent that the club could keep faith with a man who had committed such a crime. He explained that he had now dumped his season ticket and would not be going back to Chelsea because of the stand they had taken. What I would say to him now is this: if he had known the full story, then maybe his view might have been different. And you shouldn't lose everything you have worked for in life because of one mistake.

When anyone leaves, either a coach or player, the squad have a ceremonial goodbye. We form a circle with our arms round each other's shoulders and have a minute's silence. We had just started our one for Graham when Michael Duberry stopped us. 'It should be 30 seconds, not a minute,' said Doobs. 'Why?' I asked. 'Because he only got six months, not a year,' said Doobs.

But on a more serious note I honestly don't think that losing Graham made the difference between us winning one of the trophies we were contesting and just failing to land one of them. Of course we missed him. He is a bloody good coach. But we had someone ready to come in and help out Luca and that was Ray Wilkins. Ray knows the club inside out and was a great favourite here when he was a player. He is respected and knows his football. It was a bonus for us having someone with that Chelsea pedigree ready to step in when Graham went to prison. No, the biggest single factor we missed was luck, pure and simple. You look at the points that were dropped, you look at the near misses – like mine in the last minute in Mallorca when Luca would surely have buried the chance; I missed. Then there was the shot I had that was heading for the net in our FA Cup replay against Manchester United before Tore Andre Flo cleared it for them. They are the moments that decide seasons.

Chapter 23

out with the old, in with the new

So it is 9.15 a.m. and Vinnie Jones and myself are on our way to training at Wimbledon. First stop, the cafe near the training ground. Breakfast is the Full Monty – eggs, bacon, sausage, chips, tea and toast. We even went through that routine before the FA Cup final back in 1988. Then it was off for a 10.30 a.m. start with the rest of the squad. Not today it isn't. It has all changed for a professional footballer eleven years on.

That routine was still part and parcel of everyday life when I first joined Chelsea. I would go with Andy Townsend to a hotel near the training ground at Harlington and have a good brekkie before training. And after training? Round to a local cafe because at that time, there was no canteen at the training ground. Glenn Hoddle changed all that. He arranged for the canteen to start up at Harlington and brought in a dietician to ensure that we started to eat the right food. The idea was right but the dietician tried, in my opinion, to do too much too soon. The players were taken aback a bit by the sudden change. When Ruud took over, it changed again and the food was more palatable for the players. There would be salad, chicken and rice and salmon, fantastic food and just right for professional athletes.

Now Luca is in charge, we have an Italian chef who does the most wonderful sauces to go with the food. What we have adopted is an Italian approach to our food. They have proved over the years to have it exactly right in matters like diet, pre-match warm-ups, the lot. It is a great diet that we are on now and we are all going to reap the benefits in the years to come. If you want to play at your peak for longer, then you have to eat the right food. If you are going to eat junk food, like we used to, then you are not going to be able to maintain the high standard for so long. It is as simple as that.

The same principles apply to our everyday training. For a start, we do a lot more stretching than we ever used to do. We have a good stretch before a training session and afterwards and Luca is very insistent on making sure we have warmed down properly. Days off? Only one – Sunday – and only then if we don't have a midweek match. If we do, then we are in for a warm down. It is a much tougher regime under Luca than it was under Ruud Gullit or Glenn Hoddle. He works everybody really hard.

In pre-season we will train mornings and afternoons with a lot of running and physical work. At lunchtime, we will go for a short sleep and then it is back for the afternoon session. That is when we work with a football. In the morning, we don't see one. During the season, there is a lot of stretching and using weights. Luca likes to do power training – power on the legs through hurdling and then weights. If there is no midweek game, Tuesday is the power day with sessions in the morning and the afternoon. More often than not, we do not see a football at all on Tuesdays. To show you how hi-tech it all is nowadays, all our performances in training are logged on to the computer of the fitness expert Antonio Pintis. Everything is on there – how much you have lifted, how far you have run and how fast you have run. Eventually, you reach a peak and the object is to keep you at that peak.

Through the season, Antonio will devise a programme to keep you at that optimum level of performance. He wants you at your best all the time and wants you to maintain that level. It certainly worked last season when our endurance and standard of performance could not be faulted. But it has been said – and I can't really argue – that we looked a little tired in our last six games or so; I think Luca will have learned from that. I believe he could have given us a day-off after European matches, particularly away games. Often we would get back at around 4 a.m. and yet he would want us in for training at 11 a.m. that day. The last thing I want to be seen to be doing is telling the manager what to do but sometimes the players would be better off, in my opinion, just staying in bed and having a good sleep. Instead, we were up, feeling knackered, having a training session and then going back home. Because the adrenalin was still pumping, sleep was impossible. Invariably – because of the cock-up with the fixture computer that I mentioned earlier – we would be travelling the next day and travelling a long way. A rest the day before would, I feel, have been better.

Luca will have more time to concentrate on management now he has decided to quit playing. That is good for him but bad for us because I feel he still has something to contribute on the pitch. I respect his decision, but I don't agree with it. As I said before, I still can't understand why he didn't put himself on the bench in our European games. He should have done. When you want someone to come on and score a goal or do something a bit special or unexpected, Luca would have been perfect. He would have been more than capable of doing that. In that semi-final of the Cup Winners' Cup against Real Mallorca, his appearance on the field would have had a huge psychological impact. He is has the ability to frighten the life out of people. I looked at our bench at times and it was full of midfield players and defenders when what we needed was someone to score a goal. Luca would have been perfect but it was his decision to manage rather than play an active role.

Life at Chelsea is certainly a lot different under him. Ten years ago, when I first arrived, the training was far more basic and pretty much the same every day. It was five-a-side, a bit of running and some pattern-of-play work before the game. Nowadays it is more varied. It is all done in a different way. It is more scientific. Everything is done for a reason and we certainly finish training a lot later. It used to be finished at lunchtime and everyone was off. Two-session days are not unusual now while days off certainly are. But no one is complaining and I want to make that very clear. With the money that is being earned by many of the top players, they have to be truly professional athletes. It is our job and we get paid good wages to be in the best of condition to do that job properly and to the best of our ability. If that means less leisure time than we used to get, so be it. There are a lot of people outside the game who are not happy with the money we earn but I challenge anyone to turn down cash if it is offered to them. If you asked for this, this and this and your employer agreed to give it to you, don't tell me you would say no. I don't know anyone who would. And, if anyone thought they were being overpaid, would they go in to their employers and offer to give it back? Of course they wouldn't.

Footballers tend to be a target for criticism about their wages because, as I see it, they are easy targets and because for so long it has been the game of the people. Emmanuel Petit of Arsenal said last season that, yes, he earns good money but so do pop stars and actors and many other people in the entertainment business. But no one seems to have a go at them. Football is what I would call a convenient target. Obviously everyone wants to earn money and there are people in society who deserve to earn a lot more than they do at the moment. I am thinking of nurses and teachers who do a wonderful and valuable job. They deserve every penny they get and more. But it is always footballers who are dragged into the argument about people who are overpaid and what those same people who harp on about it don't realise is two important things.

Firstly, a footballer has a short career – perhaps ten years when he is at the maximum of his earning capacity. This is a big business now and you owe it to yourself and your family to earn as much as you can in that time. It is a career that doesn't last forever and you have to make sure that, when your playing days are over, you and your family are comfortable and can live okay.

Secondly, it is only a small percentage of professional players who earn what would be regarded as top money. Outsiders seem to think that every player is earning an absolute fortune but it is not like that. Just because people play for a top club, it does not mean they earn fantastic wages. Often you see wages printed in the papers and most of the time the journalist is guessing. And the guess is nearly always wrong. People like to read how much so-and-so is on and I am amazed when I see some of the figures printed. Then you hear the comments when a player makes a mistake. 'What, £50,000 a week and he can't trap a ball!' Suddenly he is crap because of a wage figure that had been bandied about and, believe me, is wrong 99 times out of a 100.

However, there are some people in football who deserve everything they get, and no one can complain about their earnings.

Chapter 24

heroes and villains

I have been fortunate to play with some talented players for club and country, but, in my mind, there is no doubt who is the best. That would be Gianfranco Zola. Quite simply, the little man is a genius. His first club in Italy was Napoli where he was the understudy to Diego Maradona. All I can say is that he is a very good learner because some of the tricks he comes up with are unbelievable. You should see him in training. He has also proved to be a great professional. When he came over here he had to learn English and adjust to a totally different culture, on and off the field. Mind you, if you listen to Luca Vialli and Roberto di Matteo, he didn't come to the club speaking very good Italian either. Franco is from the island of Sardinia where they speak with a very heavy dialect. The other Italian lads at the club always claimed they couldn't understand a word he was saying.

But the language he did speak that everyone understood was international – he could speak the language of football. From the moment we first saw him in training, we knew we had signed someone special. His control and technique were amazing – and then we saw how deadly he was at free-kicks. It was Ruud Gullit who brought him to the club and I can vividly recall his first season with us. 'Watch him now,' said Ruud. 'He is going to take some free-kicks.' We had heard all this before – but we hadn't seen anyone like Franco before. We just sat there with our mouths open. The ball was curling, dipping, doing anything he wanted it to do. 'Bloody Hell,' I remember saying. 'There is one tactic for us from now on – win free-kicks at the edge of the area.'

I have never seen anyone like him from that situation, anywhere around the penalty area.

He is deadly, that is the only word for it. I reckon four out of five beat the goalkeeper while 19 out of 20 are on target. That is how good and accurate he is. He is also a really nice bloke who cares about his football and cares about people. He also knows how to look after himself on the pitch, an instinct that he developed in Italy where strikers get so little space in which to work. Basically, you can't get near him. He is so quick and he is so nimble with such a sharp football brain. In training sessions we have one-to-one situations and I would always dread it if I was up against Franco – mind you, so did everyone else. You just couldn't get the ball off him because you couldn't get within a yard of him. It must be a nightmare for the opposition. If you are left in a situation where it is just you and him, you know you are in trouble.

I apologise if my way of containing Franco sounds crude but I know what I would do to stop him if I was in the opposite team: I would just have to boot him. There is nothing legal you can do to keep him quiet when he is on form. Mind you, you have to get close enough to do that first and that is by no means easy. He makes space and uses his razor-sharp brain so well that you struggle to get that close. But he is a rare talent and it has been a privilege for me to play alongside him. He gets so upset when we lose and really takes it to heart if he feels he has been in any way responsible.

A nice guy is Franco – and he also happens to be a world-class talent. The young lads at the club can't fail to learn from watching and working with a player like that. It will do them good in the long run and shows what can be achieved if they watch him like he obviously watched the great Maradona. They just have to look and learn. And, if one of those kids turns out half as good as him, they will have done well. He is a modest man who loves his family and loves his football. It was a great day's work when we brought him to the club.

The most gifted player that I have played against is Paul Gascoigne. He also happens to be one of the biggest characters that English football has produced in recent years and, although he has often been in the public eye for the wrong reasons, there is no doubting his talent. Of his generation of English players he was the best. He had natural ability and that was there for everyone to see. But in England you also need to be strong – and, believe me, Gazza was strong. The way he used his arms was really clever.

I know a lot of people accused him of trying to elbow opponents but that really wasn't the case and I speak as someone who often was one of those opponents. He would put his arm across you while he was in possession and that would enable him to block your run, help him to keep the ball and make sure that you were always off balance if you tried to make a challenge. I can't think of any other English player who was as strong as Gazza at running with the ball. He also enjoyed himself on the pitch. He clearly has a great love of football and a huge personality that gives him genuine presence out there. Yes, he likes a laugh but he has never let anyone take liberties with him. He was the perfect English player of his time – with strength, speed, the ability to go past people and the knack of scoring exceptional goals.

I know some people think it is sad that he is now past his best and for one reason or another cannot reproduce the kind of football he did, say, ten years ago. But I don't feel sad at all where Gazza is concerned. Why? Because we were lucky to see the best of him, we were lucky to see Gazza in his prime. Maybe we could have had a couple more years but a series of bad injuries put paid to that. But we still saw vintage Gazza – at his strongest and his most lethal – and that is what I will always remember.

There was a chance at one time that we could have been teammates at club level. Glenn Hoddle tried to sign him on loan when he was at Glasgow Rangers and that was one hell of a prospect. It would have been great for him and great for Chelsea, but the move never worked out. That was a shame. To play alongside a player of his skill and presence on a regular basis would have been great for me. I would have relished that – and it would certainly have made a welcome change from trying to contend with his bloody arms going across me all the time I was trying to tackle him.

When it comes to the best manager I worked for, it's a difficult choice. I have already put on record my admiration for Terry Venables, a real players' man. He was loyal to the men who worked for him and he stood by me when I had my troubles with the taxi driver. That counts for a lot in my book.

But I would have to give my vote to Bobby Gould. He took over a different club, one like no other in the top flight when he arrived at Wimbledon as the successor to Harry Bassett. It needed a special kind of man to make sure that the foundations laid by Harry were not disturbed. And that man was Gouldie. He was great on spirit and team spirit was what made Wimbledon tick. Instead of trying to change everything when he came in like some managers do, he encouraged the approach and attitude that Harry had fostered in his years at the club. He was also one of the most straight and honest people with whom I have ever had to deal. Yes, we had our rows and our rucks – not least when I was asking for a transfer on a daily basis and he just screwed up my letters, grinned and threw them in the bin. But he was straightforward and let the players know where they stood. They liked him for that. A lot of people – on the outside, I might add, people who don't know Gouldie – have given him stick over the years but very rarely has that criticism been levelled by the players who worked with him. He also pulled off a master-stroke when he appointed Don Howe as coach.

The minute those two left, the club seemed to go down a bit. Gouldie's great strength was his knowledge of players in the lower divisions. He knew Wimbledon couldn't pay big transfer fees, he knew they would never be able to compete on a regular basis with the rich clubs – or indeed the not-so-rich clubs. So he had to unearth his prospects from the Second and Third Divisions. And he did it so well with the likes of Terry Phelan, Keith Curle and John Scales. They were to earn Wimbledon a fortune in the years to come and basically make sure that the club survived even though they were getting gates lower than many First and even some Second Division sides. In Don he had the master of set pieces. Don would work and work us until we got it right. He was also excellent at putting over his ideas. No one was ever in any doubt about what he wanted.

Another of Gouldie's strengths was knowing just when to give players a lift. To the outside world he may have seemed somewhat eccentric but he had this knack of doing the right thing at the right time. It wasn't unusual for him to walk in, point to three different players and say, 'You, you and you – new contracts. You deserve them.' For some of us, that money meant a lot because Wimbledon could never afford to be among the best payers in the league. Yes, I had my rows with him and quite often we were at loggerheads. But there was a mutual respect between us and, whenever I see him now, we inevitably end up having a long chat. He is a good bloke is Gouldie.

But there is no doubt in my mind when it comes to nominating the hardest person I have ever faced. It has to be Jimmy Case, who played for Liverpool, Brighton and Southampton. I came across him when he was at Southampton and I was at Wimbledon. I thought I was jack-the-lad but he soon put me in my place. Now I am not the biggest guy in the world but over the years – because of the environment where I grew up and through the football I have played – I have learned to look after myself. No one had really frightened me . . . until I came up against Jimmy Case. After the game, I said to myself that I would never go near him again. I had tried to give him a whack and I got it back with interest. I decided not to go down that road again.

The following season we were down at The Dell again. My good mate Vaughan Ryan was in the Wimbledon team and Case was in the Southampton line-up. I warned him beforehand, 'Don't go near Jimmy Case. He is one hard man. He nearly cut me in half last time I faced him.' Did Vaughan listen? Did he hell. He was very naive and thought he was tougher than Jimmy Case. He gave him a bit of stick and Case just whacked him – and broke his jaw. Not only was his jaw in a bad way, so was Vaughan. He was out of it, in a daze and totally disorientated. He didn't know where he was or what he was doing – and that showed up in the game in hilarious fashion. We got the ball and started attacking only for Vaughan to be running the other way. Then

Southampton got the ball and were attacking our goal – and Vaughan was just running past them in the opposite direction. When we attacked he was defending and, when we were defending, he decided to attack.

He was all over the place and even he was laughing when we all watched the video later. Vaughan needed to have an operation to wire up his jaw – and all because he wouldn't listen. Jimmy Case was one hard man and Vaughan found out the hard way.

Chapter 25

dennis the menace

When I was younger, a defeat used to drive me mad and I used to take it home with me after the game. I used to go over and over what had happened in my mind. But over the years, I have found I have been able to handle it much better. Rule one: never let it affect a good night out. Of course it hurts but in recent years I have stopped going home and sulking about things.

In fact, Saturday night isn't really too much of a problem. If things have gone wrong it's the following day, when you start reading the papers, that it really hurts. Although I cope much better these days, there was one incident which will always haunt me – that last-minute miss with the header against Real Mallorca in the Cup Winners' Cup semi-final. I so wanted to score after all the hassle I had from the first leg. I thought I had done everything right but the ball went inches wide. I must have replayed that header 5,000 times in my head. But even things like that don't drive me mad like they used to. As I have got older I can handle that better. You can drive yourself mad if you keep thinking about things that have happened that you wish hadn't.

Away from football I go out with a small circle of friends that have become close to me over the years – people I have grown up with or become friends with. But not pop stars or celebrities – that isn't for me. I have mates like Jim Creed, Andrew Dale, Vaughan Ryan, Gary Britnell and, of course, the lovely lady in my life, Claire.

They are the people I spend time with between games. We go out and have a few beers and usually end up at Roberto di Matteo's restaurant, Friends, for a meal. We just sit there, eat well and relax. It's not usually a problem if I'm recognised. Of course, you get the odd sarcastic remark; someone will invariably shout out 'Taxi' when they see me. It's a bit sad really because they think they are the only people to have joked about it. I just wish I had a pound for every time someone has said it, I would be mega-wealthy. But basically, I just let my hair down a bit with people who are very special to me. We enjoy ourselves and don't cause any problems. I am part of close-knit group and we have a bit of fun. I am with people I have known a long time and that ensures my feet stay on the ground and you don't get above yourself. I stick with people I have known for years. You do that and, in my experience, you can't go wrong.

I've always liked jokes and pranks. Fortunately, I can't think of any occasions when I have been on the receiving end. Why? I think people are too frightened about the revenge I will get on them. Whatever they do to me, they will get it back with interest . . . and they know it. None of the stunts I pull are meant to be malicious or are intended to hurt anyone. They are just to make life a bit more colourful – although I am not so sure Gianfranco Zola or Glenn Hoddle saw the funny side of a couple of my pranks.

Franco is a lovely bloke – he wouldn't harm a fly and would not think ill of anyone. So when he was reading a book in English to improve his grasp of the language, he did not suspect a thing when I kept asking him about it. 'What is that book?' I'd say. 'Is a spy book, a thriller . . . you know, Wisey, a mystery,' he answered. Every time I saw him his head was buried in this book and I'd always ask him about it. 'Yes, is a good book,' he said. After about the tenth time, he is such a lovely bloke that he said, 'Wisey, you are interested in this book, yes? I will buy you one for yourself. Is a good book.'

What he didn't know was that I had a plan. When he left the book down one day, I managed to tear out the last chapter. Then our regular chats resumed. 'How is it, the book?' I would always say. 'Very good, very exciting. I can't wait to find out what 'appen in the end' was his reply every time I asked – until one day he wasn't reading it any more.

'Finished the book, Franco?' I asked. 'How was it, a good story?' 'For long time, yes,' he replied. 'But Wisey, the ending, it was strange, very strange.' I couldn't hold it back any longer and just burst out laughing. Then I explained what I had done and all he could say was 'Bastard, you bastard'. Anyway, I promised him he could have the chapter I had torn out back if he scored in our next game against Crystal Palace. And he did.

Then there was the time myself and John Spencer had Glenn Hoddle in a real panic. It was when Glenn was player-manager and needed treatment for an injury. At great expense the club had bought a huge oxygen bubble contraption to help with injuries. You get inside it and the oxygen is supposed to accelerate the healing process, especially for muscle injuries. Glenn was inside this transparent con-traption and the physiotherapist at the time, Bob Ward, had left him in there to attend to someone else. Myself and John Spencer saw the potential of this situation and we crawled along the floor, both carrying bath towels, so Glenn couldn't see us from inside the 'bubble'. Suddenly we threw the towels over the bubble so that it went dark inside and we scampered out, turning the light off on the way.

Glenn was in a right panic and looked really upset when Bob finally came back to see how he was getting on with the treatment. He had got really claustrophobic and was in a right state. Spenny and me were in fits, though.

I know I will never be regarded as a footballer for the purists. I accept that. I also know that I have made perhaps more than the occasional mistake in my career. But with me, I would like to think that what you see is what you get. I have been lucky, but on many occasions I have made my own luck. If I had to use one word to describe myself, it would be a fighter. I have had to fight for everything I have ever won and achieved in football and I see no need to apologise for that. I work hard, bloody hard. I always have done and always will do. That is the type of person I am.

I have not been blessed with the individual skills of other people, the natural ability of someone like Paul Gascoigne, Franco Zola or Luca

Vialli. But I compensate for that by trying hard and my attitude to the work ethic is probably better than many other footballers I can think of. I have been given what they call in football a great engine, which means I can run all day, which again seems to be beyond some other players. I am not that quick but I am sharp. I can see things happening on a pitch and I can read them.

I have never been the tallest player on the pitch but my dad toughened me up very early. He would play me as an 11-year-old against kids four years older. Believe me, when you are involved in football in the area of London where I was born, you harden up very quickly. You have to survive. Sometimes I would play against my dad and his mates on a red shale surface and on more than one occasion I got booted up in the air. Jim Creed, a friend of me and my dad's, did it once and I could see that he was worried that my dad would come over and give him a right-hander. But my dad knew that, with my size, if I was going to survive in football, I would have to learn to take knocks, so he said and did nothing. Me? I just got up and got on with the game. It was no good being a cry-baby, you just had to handle that sort of thing. It was all part of the learning process, you just had to look after yourself. There was no option, not in the White City and Notting Hill areas. Around there they play hard and they play to win. More often than not it is a question of the survival of the fittest and the strongest. If you are weak, if you can't handle the knocks, you soon get found out. There were threats all the time and, if you responded, if you wanted to take the fella up on it, then you had better be prepared to see it through because in football round there no one backs down. If you don't mean it, then don't say it – just get on with it.

I honestly don't think I am what you would call a dirty player. I am hard but I am fair. I won't let anyone take liberties with me, though. If someone does something to me, then I will get my own back. That is the way it was when I was growing up and that is the way it is now. And, no, I don't care how big they are.

It used to be said that Wimbledon were at their most effective in the days before television became so involved and was able to analyse every kick, tackle and incident that happened during a game. To put it bluntly, yes, in the old days you used to be able to get away with a lot more. Quite simply, these days you can't. In my days at Wimbledon they had characters like John Fashanu and Vinnie Jones and during the course of the game they would get involved in some pretty physical clashes. But that wasn't new. Ron 'Chopper' Harris at Chelsea was a great favourite with the home fans, as were players like David Webb and Billy Bremner at Chelsea and Leeds.

They were genuine characters who got totally involved and the crowds loved to see them play. They would crash into people, the game went on and nothing was said or done. I can recall seeing a video of the 1970 FA Cup final replay between Chelsea and Leeds and seeing Ron Harris send Eddie Gray right up in the air. Free-kick, nothing more and no one complained.

But that kind of personality isn't there any more. They have been forced out of football. The press loved them because they loved to write about that kind of character and the fans loved to read about them. But, the way the game has gone, those characters have almost all disappeared. Nobody can do those things now. You step out of line twice and you are off. Clubs don't really want players like that but the best teams need people like that, players who will put their foot in. Look at Roy Keane, for example.

These days there are no secrets and, largely because of television, everything is scrutinised. Now you will get done if something is picked up by the cameras, even if the referee misses it. If television shows it, the FA will act. Graeme Le Saux suffered like that in 1999 after the Premiership game with Liverpool, while I was charged by UEFA, although subsequently cleared, after the 'biting' incident against Real Mallorca. Personally, I think that, if the referee doesn't take any action, that should be it. I don't think it's right that television should be able to put you in the dock. I sometimes go to watch Sunday morning football and, believe me, if the referee saw everything, the games would never finish. He usually misses half of what goes on. If he saw it all, there would be no players left on the pitch. What it boils down to, in my opinion, is this: any action should be down to what the referee reports on the day and not as a result of television or press reports.

So many match reports are about controversial incidents and so few about how good or bad the game was. You rarely read about a great goal, great pass or superb save. It's always about a tackle missed by the referee or an allegation that something happened in the tunnel, anything but the game. What I have to accept, though, is that that is what people want to read. They seem to want controversy.

So, when television took away the secrets, they took away a lot of what made Wimbledon successful. That team are always going to carry the 'Crazy Gang' tag but, to be honest, for me that all went a few years ago.

Off the pitch I am totally different, although that wasn't always the case. I got into trouble when I was 18 over what you would call nowadays a 'road rage' incident. I was driving through Shepherd's Bush when someone pulled out in front of me – no warning, nothing. I was furious and started flashing my lights at him. He just sped off but along a stretch of road near the tube station there is a series of traffic lights. They turned to red as he reached them and I pulled up behind him, got out of my car and told him to get out. He wouldn't – and then he sped off making a sign at me like he was, let's say, shuffling dice. Before he got away from where I was standing I was able to give his car a kick and I dented a panel. I thought that was going to be the end of it until a few minutes later when a police car pulled me over, I was charged with causing criminal damage and got fined £450 in court. I learned my lesson – for ten years or so anyway.

I don't take any grudges into the after-match scene either. Once we come off the field (and, I suppose, clear the tunnel area) I bear no grudges. You might recall that I had a run-in with Nicky Butt of Manchester United while we were coming off at Old Trafford once but, as far as I am concerned, it is over with. If I saw him when I was out, I would happily buy him a beer. No problem.

For any faults that people might think I have, they can never say that I lack determination and I am sure that attitude was fashioned in my early years when I had those knockbacks at Southampton. They weren't expected and they weren't welcome but I learned from them and in the long run they did me no harm at all. In fact, they gave me an edge and I was even keener to succeed. At the time it hurt – show me someone who isn't hurt by rejection. But you handle it, you take it on board and you set out to make the most of any other opportunity that comes your way. And I did that with Wimbledon.

All I ever wanted to do with my life was play football, and I got there. I learned to take nothing for granted and that you have to work hard to get anywhere in life. Perhaps I did assume everything would come right when I was younger and, when it didn't, I just had to learn to cope. But cope I did and now I am reaping the benefits of that. Yes, I know people can criticise me for my disciplinary record – and one fan did recently. He dropped a letter into my house after my sending-off against Oxford in the FA Cup match. He said I was a capable footballer playing in a wonderful team. Then he said I had a big mouth and missed too many matches because of suspension, and that it was hard to justify the wages I was being paid because of it. In short, he went right into one and clearly didn't rate me that highly. Fair enough, he's entitled to his point of view. But he didn't have the guts to put his name and address on the letter so I could send him reply, and he had the cheek to leave the letter at my house when he knew I would be out. That took a lot of guts. At least if I have something to say to someone I will say it to their face. Posting a letter and then running off is not my style and never will be.

What I will reassure that gentleman about is that my heart and soul is at Chelsea. As far as I am concerned, I want to spend the rest of my career here as a player. I honestly can't envisage going anywhere else. The club means everything to me. I feel so proud that I have played a part in the way it has grown since I turned up to sign from Wimbledon all those years ago. Gone are those ramshackle offices. The stadium is one of the best in the country now and there are all the trappings of success around the place. And not least, we have a team to be proud of, a team that has given the supporters back their pride in Chelsea. When finishing third, in what is arguably the hardest league in Europe to win, becomes a disappointment, then you know that progress is being made. We have top-class players and the facilities are getting better all the time. Now the important thing is to keep on with that improvement and I very much want to be part of that process.

It is often said – and wrongly – that the spirit at a club like ours, with so many different nationalities, cannot be that great. Nothing could be further from the truth. Yes, we have a real collection of overseas players from Italy, Norway, Romania, Nigeria, France, Denmark, Spain and Holland. But the feeling of togetherness is evident throughout Chelsea. We couldn't have achieved what we have done without it. Everyone at the club understands what is being said because they all have some understanding of English. There is no communication problem.

It starts at the top with Luca. He has a tremendous sense of humour to go with his shrewd tactical brain. He will get his point across and still have time for a laugh. There was one occasion when he was using sketches on a huge board to illustrate a point. On the top sheet he was showing what he wanted to happen at a certain set piece. 'They will expect us to do this,' he said, indicating that the opposition will expect the ball to be passed to a wide player for the ball to be whipped over into the goalmouth. 'But we will do this,' he said, saying the ball should be laid square to me for a shot. 'And then this will happen,' he said – and turned over the next page . . . where there was a picture of where my shot had gone. Top corner? No chance. He had drawn it hitting the corner flag. The rest of the squad just cracked up. It was a double-edged exercise. He had made a serious point and at the same time brought a smile to everyone's face. And just because the lads come from abroad, it does not mean we don't have characters among them. Gus Poyet is certainly one. He is a great influence in the dressing room and Gianfranco Zola is also a very funny little chap – and the subject of a song composed by Michael Duberry, hated by him and just loved by Luca.

When Franco first arrived, the Chelsea punters soon had a song for him. It was to the tune of 'Yellow Submarine' and went like this:

There's a man from Italy,
And he's only five foot three,
And when he scores we all sing,
Gianfranco is the king.
We all agree, Gianfranco is the king.

Doobs decided to change the lyrics. He came up with a new version and we told the rest of the lads about it. Dan Petrescu, Gus and the rest of them were desperate to learn it. They did. Franco was introduced to it while we were sitting round in a circle for a session of stretching at training. We have to stretch individually, and, when it was Franco's turn, Doobs suddenly said, 'Let's have a song for Franco.' So there we all were on a sunny day at the training ground with Luca watching. Then came the new chorus and you have to bear in mind that Franco has got quite big teeth:

There's a man from Italy,
And he's got a set of teeth,
And when he smiles we all run,
Gianfranco is Red Rum.
We all agree, Gianfranco is Red Rum.

Not surprisingly, Franco hates it. And not surpisingly, we sing it all the more. Every time he says 'Oh no, please, not that', we just sing it louder and Luca loves it. You don't get that sort of camaraderie at a club where there is no spirit.

As for the long term, well I would like to stay in football. I have worked for many managers at club and international level. From each of them I have tried to learn something and one day I hope to be able to put what I've learned into practice. But management? I don't know. Despite what you might think, I would hate upsetting people by leaving them out of the team. I know how that feels and, believe me, it is not a nice feeling. Coaching would be more likely, hopefully in some capacity at Chelsea. This place has become part of my life.

career highlights

1966

Born in Kensington, on 16 December, to Dennis and Pam Wise.

1979

Spotted by a Southampton scout, Dennis begins training at their centre in Slough.

1981

Signs for Southampton on Associated Schoolboy forms.

Appears on *Record Breakers* after his team wins a national under-fifteen five-a-side competition held at Wembley Arena. The young Dennis announces his intention to become a professional footballer and win the FA Cup.

1982

Selected for trials for the England Schoolboy team, Dennis is among four players dropped after their rowdy behaviour on a train is reported.

After being suspended from school, Dennis leaves school early to start his apprenticeship at Southampton.

1985

Signs for Wimbledon as a professional in March after being released by Southampton. Plays his first game as a substitute against Cardiff two months later and comes on to set up the winning goal.

1986

Full debut against Sheffield Wednesday. Wimbledon win promotion to the old First Division. Dennis scores his first goal against Charlton and becomes a first team regular.

1988

Scores the winner in the FA Cup semi-final against Luton and sets up the winning goal in the FA Cup final against Liverpool, delivering an inch-perfect free-kick to Lawrie Sanchez to head home. Wimbledon's win is one of the biggest upsets in football history.

Voted Wimbledon Player of the Year.

1989

Despite his requests for a transfer, Wimbledon will not release Dennis.

Selected for the England squad for the Rous Cup. He makes it to the substitutes bench for the match against Chilie but does not play.

1990

Signs for Chelsea for £1.6 million, a record for the club. Plays his debut against Derby at Stamford Bridge in August. Later that month, in his third game for Chelsea, he is sent off after a tackle on Andy Gray of Crystal Palace.

1991

Selected for the England squad by Graham Taylor, Dennis makes his England debut in the Euro 1992 qualifier against Turkey and scores the winning goal. He also plays for his country in the friendly against

Russia and joins the England squad on a tour to the Far East, Australia and New Zealand, playing in two games against New Zealand and coming on as a substitute against Australia.

1992

Dennis makes his 100th appearance for Chelsea against Walsall in the Coca-Cola Cup.

1993

Dennis is appointed Chelsea captain by new manager Glenn Hoddle and signs a new contract with Chelsea.

1994

Captains Chelsea in the FA Cup final against Manchester United. United win 4–0.

Dennis gains three more England caps in games against Norway, Romania and Nigeria.

In October, Dennis is arrested after an altercation with a taxi driver. Hoddle takes his captaincy from him. During a match against Liverpool he suffers a severe thigh injury.

1995

Found guilty of assault, Dennis is sentenced to three months imprisonment but freed, pending an appeal. As a result of the conviction, he is dropped from the England squad for their match against the Republic of Ireland. The conviction is overturned on appeal. He returns to the England squad later in the year in matches against Columbia, Norway and Portugal.

Dennis makes his 200th appearance for Chelsea against Newcastle in September.

1996

Scores his 50th goal for Chelsea in February, his first of two goals during a league match against Southampton.

Dennis plays for England against Hungary in the build up to Euro '96 but is dropped from the final squad for the competition.

1997

Captains Chelsea to FA Cup victory and lifts their first trophy in 26 years.

1998

Plays his 300th game for Chelsea against Southampton in January.

Leads Chelsea to victory in the Coca-Cola Cup, Cup Winners' Cup and European Super Cup, making him the most successful captain in Chelsea's history.

Chelsea Player of the Year.

1999-2000

Testimonial year at Chelsea. 0-0 draw with Venezia nets record testimonial payout to a Chelsea player.

Leads Chelsea to victory in the FA Cup Final and their Champions League campaign, culminating in a quarter-final defeat by Barcelona.

Wins several more England caps following a well deserved recall to the national squad including an inspirational performance against Brazil.

career statistics

Up to the end of the 1998/99 season

Born: 16 December, 1966, Kensington
Height: 169 cm (5′ 6½″)
Weight: 69kg (10st, 12lbs)

Appearances Year-by-Year

1984/85
League appearances: (1)

1985/86
League appearancess: 1 (+ 3)

1986/87
League appearances: 25 (+3), goals: 4
FA Cup appearances: 1
League Cup appearances: 2

1987/88
League appearances: 29 (+1), goals: 10
FA Cup appearances: 6, goals: 2
League Cup appearances: 2

1988/89

League appearances: 37, goals: 5

FA Cup appearances: 3, goals: 1

League Cup appearances: 5

Charity Shield appearance: 1

1989/90

League appearances: 35, goals: 8

FA Cup appearances: 1

League Cup appearances: 5

1990/91

League appearances: 33, goals: 10

FA Cup appearances: 1

League Cup appearances: 7, goals: 2

Full Members Cup appearances: 1, goals: 1

International appearances: 4 (+1), goals 1

1991/92

League appearances: 37 (+1), goals: 10

FA Cup appearances 4, goals: 2

League Cup appearances: 2, goals: 1

Full Members Cup appearances: 4, goals: 1

1992/93

League appearances: 27, goals: 3

League Cup appearances: 5, goals: 1

1993/94

League appearances: 35, goals: 4

FA Cup appearances: 4

League Cup appearances: 2, goals: 2

International appearances: 1

1994/95

League appearances: 18 (+1), goals: 6

FA Cup appearances: 2

League Cup appearances: 3

European Cup Winners' Cup appearances: 5, goals 1

International appearances: 1 (+1)

1995/96

League appearances: 34 (+1), goals: 7

FA Cup appearances: 7, goals: 1

League Cup appearances: 2

International appearances: 3 (+1)

1996/97

League appearances: 27 (+4), goals: 3

FA Cup appearances: 7, goals: 3

League Cup appearances: 2

1997/98

League appearances: 26, goals: 3

League Cup appearances: 4

Charity Shield appearance: 1

European Cup Winners' Cup appearances: 9

1998/99

League appearances: 21 (+1)

FA Cup appearances: 5, goals: 1

League Cup appearances: 2

European Cup Winners' Cup appearances: 8, goals: 1

1999/2000

League appearances: 29 (+1), goals: 4

FA Cup appearances: 5, goals: 2

Champions League appearances: 14 (+1), goals: 4

Totals

Wimbledon
League appearances: 128 (+4), goals: 27
FA Cup appearances: 11, goals: 3
League Cup appearances: 14
Charity Shield appearances: 1

Chelsea
League appearances: 287 (+9), goals: 50
FA Cup appearances: 35, goals: 9
League Cup appearances: 29, goals: 6
Full Members Cup appearances: 5, goals: 2
Charity Shield appearances: 1
European Cup Winners' Cup appearances: 22, goals: 2
Champions League appearances: 14 (+1), goals: 4

England
Appearances: 9 (+3), seven wins and five draws, goals: 1

Honours
Wimbledon
FA Cup winners medal 1988
Wimbledon Player of the Year 1988
Charity Shield runners up medal 1988

Chelsea
FA Cup runners up medal 1994
FA Cup winners medal 1997, 2000
Charity Shield runners up medal 1997
Coca-Cola Cup winners medal 1998
European Cup Winners' Cup winners medal 1998
European Super Cup winners medal 1998
Chelsea Player of the Year 1998

England
12 caps
3 England B caps
1 Under-21 cap

index